D0409963

Lakeland and Bauer Media Ltd hereby exclude all liability to the extent permitted by law for any errors or omission in this book and for any loss, damage or expense (whether direct or indirect) suffered by a third party relying on any information contained in this book.

This book was created in 2015 for Lakeland by AWW Books, an imprint of Octopus Publishing Group Ltd, based on materials licensed to it by Bauer Media Books, Sydney.

Bauer Media Limited
54 Park St, Sydney
GPO Box 4088, Sydney, NSW 2001
www.awwcookbooks.com.au

OCTOPUS PUBLISHING GROUP
Design – Chris Bell
Food Director – Pamela Clark

Published for Lakeland in the United Kingdom by Octopus Publishing Group Limited

Carmelite House
50 Victoria Embankment
London EC4Y 0DZ
United Kingdom
phone + 44 (0) 207 632 5400;
fax + 44 (0) 207 632 5405
aww@octopusbooks.co.uk;
www.octopusbooks.co.uk
www.australian-womens-weekly.com

Printed and bound in China

A catalogue record for this book is available from the British Library.

ISBN 978-1-909770-31-7

© Bauer Media Limited 2015
ABN 18 053 273 546
This publication is copyright. No part of it may be reproduced or transmitted in any form without the written permission of the Publisher.

This book includes dishes made with nuts and nut derivatives. It is advisable for those with known allergic reactions to nuts and nut derivatives and those who may be potentially vulnerable to these allergies, such as pregnant and nursing mothers, invalids, the elderly, babies and children to avoid dishes made with nuts and nut oils. It is also prudent to check the labels of pre-prepared ingredients for the possible inclusion of nut derivatives.

Some of the recipes in this book have appeared in other publications.

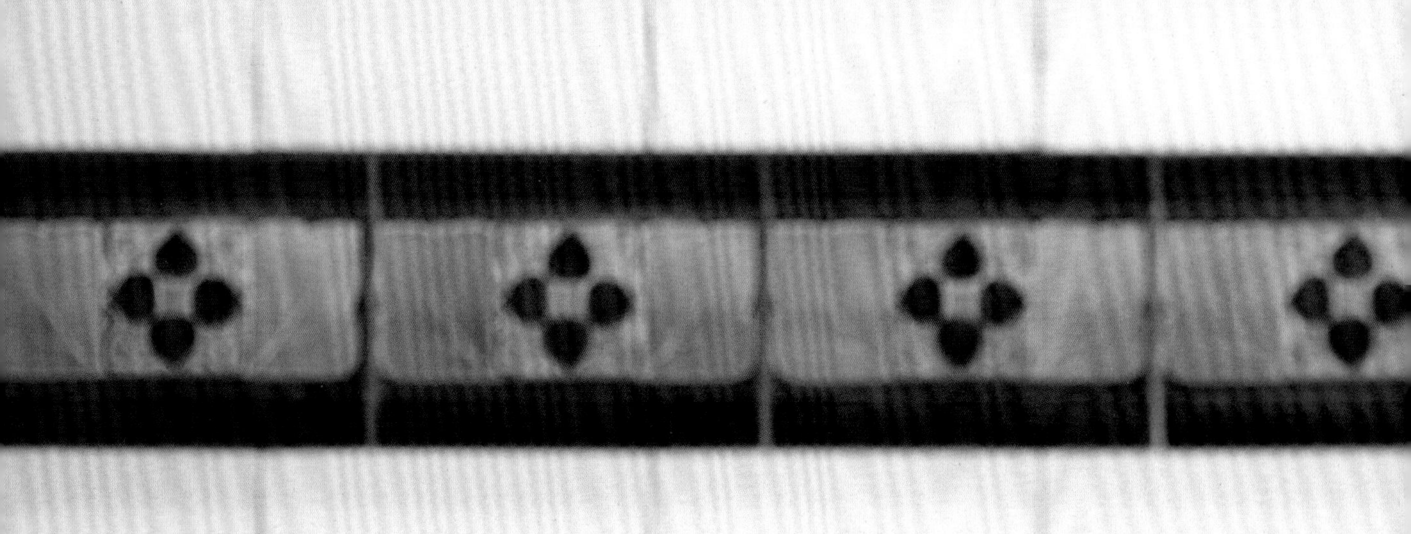

# SLOW COOKER

This collection of 56 delicious, prep-now-eat-later recipes is ideal for all busy cooks. It offers classic favourites, like Cauliflower Cheese and Lancashire Hot Pot, alongside exciting new dishes, including Coconut Curried Beef and Spanish Caramel Rice Pudding. Every recipe is accompanied by a beautiful colour photograph to inspire you to get into the kitchen and get cooking.

With every recipe triple-tested® for perfect results, this excellent cookbook is sure to be one of the best-loved on your kitchen bookshelf. To discover the rest of our range of cookbooks, together with our unrivalled selection of creative kitchenware, visit one of our friendly Lakeland stores or shop online at www.lakeland.co.uk.

# Contents

# *Introduction*

**GETTING THE BEST FROM YOUR SLOW COOKER**

**There's nothing quite as comforting as the delicious aroma of a slow-cooked meal and slow cookers are hard to beat for convenience too. Here are some pointers for getting the best from your slow cooker.**

### FIRST STEPS

Slow cookers are available in a wide range of shapes and sizes and with a variety of features. Some have a 'warm' or 'auto' setting that does not cook your food but, instead, is designed to keep the cooked food at the right temperature until you are ready to eat.

The first step before turning on your slow cooker is to read the manufacturer's instructions thoroughly to familiarise yourself with its features, the settings for operating it and the all-important safety measures

### SLOW COOKER SAFETY

- Always read the manufacturer's instructions for your particular slow cooker before you begin using it.
- The metal components of a slow cooker get very hot so ensure no one touches them while the cooker is on.
- Make sure your slow cooker is sitting securely on a flat surface, away from water, any heat sources and out of reach of children or pets.
- The cord should be well away from water or heat sources and positioned so that there is no danger of it getting caught up on anything.
- Do not put frozen ingredients in the slow cooker; defrost meat and poultry thoroughly in the refrigerator before slow cooking.
- Never submerge the base of the slow cooker in water.

### WHAT CAN I USE THE SLOW COOKER FOR?

Slow cookers can be used to make a host of delicious dishes from soups, stews, sauces and casseroles to curries, roasts and puddings.

Cheaper, tougher cuts of red meat are perfect for slow cookers. The long, slow cooking time will tenderise cuts and the flavours will be mouthwatering. Stewing meats such as venison, goat, rabbit and mutton are also great for slow cooking.

All kinds of poultry work well in the slow cooker but pieces on the bones, such as drumsticks, work best. The most important thing to remember is not to overcook poultry as this will make it dry and stringy.

Generally, seafood is not suitable for use in a slow cooker as it toughens quickly.

**SAVE MONEY**

Using your slow cooker will get the most from cheaper cuts like beef brisket, pork and lamb shoulder, and chicken thighs.

### THE TRICK FOR FLAVOURSOME MEAT

While slow cookers are all about simply adding your ingredients and letting the cooker do the rest, browning the meat before it is added to the cooker will make all the difference.

Using a large, heated and oiled frying pan, add the meat in small batches and turn every so often to make sure it browns evenly. Make sure the pan is over a medium-high heat and that there is enough oil otherwise the meat will stew, rather than caramelise.

## A WORD ABOUT FAT

Slow cooking can result in a lot of fat being extracted. The best way to remove the fat before serving is to refrigerate the cooked food. The fat will then sit on the top and can be easily skimmed off before the food is gently reheated for serving. If you want to serve the meal straightaway, then a simple but effective technique is to wait about half an hour for the dish to settle and the fat to rise then carefully dip in paper towel to soak up the visible fat or use a shallow spoon to gently skim it off.

## PLANNING AHEAD

If you want to turn your slow cooker on first thing in the morning, a little planning goes a long way. If you're short of time in the morning, the night before you can cut and trim any meat, chop any vegetables, measure out dry ingredients and prepare any sauce. Refrigerate the components in separate, sealable containers and in the morning all you need to do is add them to the slow cooker and turn it on. You can even brown your meat and put it in a sealable container, along with juices, in the refrigerator, ready for the next day.

### MAXIMISE FLAVOUR

Take the time to brown meat really well before it goes in the slow cooker to improve flavour and appearance.

## CLEANING YOUR SLOW COOKER

Always check the manufacturer's instructions for your particular model, but here are some basic tips:

- The slow cooker insert can be washed in hot, soapy water and most are dishwasher-safe.
- Soaking the slow cooker insert in warm water and then scrubbing with a nylon or plastic brush will help remove any cooked-on food.
- To clean the outside of your slow cooker, simply wipe it down with a damp cloth and then dry.
- Avoid using abrasive scourers or cleaners as these can damage the surface of your slow cooker.
- Never place a hot insert into cold water as this can cause the insert to break.

### KEEP THE LID ON

Resist the temptation to lift the lid of your slow cooker to check how things are going; the dish will cook much better if you don't.

## ADAPTING YOUR FAVOURITE RECIPES

Many of your favourite soup, stew and curry recipes can be adapted for the slow cooker, even if you are not used to cooking them this way. You may need to adjust the amount of liquid you add to take into account the long, slow cooking time but, with a little experimentation, there are endless possibilities. As a general rule of thumb, when trying out casseroles, tagines, curries and so on in your slow cooker, put the vegetables in first, then the meat and, finally, add the liquid.

### HEALTHY ADDITIONS

Bulk out slow-cooked stews and soups by adding pulses like chickpeas and lentils. These are cheap, nutritious and they also count towards your five a day.

## THE RECIPES IN THIS BOOK

Each of the recipes gives the quantities for both a 1.5-litre slow cooker and a 3.5-litre slow cooker. The two lists of ingredients are clearly differentiated for ease of use and the method is the same for both sizes of cooker.

If your slow cooker is bigger than this, you can simply adapt the recipes to suit by increasing the amount of liquid and quantity of ingredients.

Each recipe also has a note about whether it is suitable to freeze and at what point in the recipe, so that you can conveniently cook now and enjoy later or cook extra to freeze.

# Soups

# Chicken mulligatawny

**for a 3.5-litre cooker:**

2 medium brown onions (300g), chopped coarsely
2 cloves garlic, chopped coarsely
2 medium carrots (240g), chopped coarsely
1 stalk celery (150g), trimmed, chopped coarsely
1 fresh red chilli, chopped coarsely
4cm piece fresh ginger (20g), grated
2 chicken leg portions (700g)
1 tablespoon mild curry powder
1 teaspoon ground cumin
1 teaspoon garam masala
750ml chicken stock
250ml coconut milk
6 tablespoons fresh coriander leaves

for a 1.5-litre cooker:

1 small brown onion (100g), chopped coarsely
1 clove garlic, chopped coarsely
1 small carrot (80g), chopped coarsely
½ stalk celery (50g), trimmed, chopped coarsely
½ fresh red chilli, chopped coarsely
2cm piece fresh ginger (10g), grated
1 chicken leg portion (230g)
2 teaspoons mild curry powder
½ teaspoon ground cumin
½ teaspoon garam masala
250ml chicken stock
85ml coconut milk
2 tablespoons fresh coriander leaves

**method:**

**1** Place onion, garlic, carrot, celery, chilli, ginger, chicken, curry powder, cumin, garam masala and stock in a slow cooker. Cook, covered, on low, for 8 hours.

**2** Carefully remove chicken from the cooker; when cool enough to handle, discard the skin and bones. Shred meat coarsely using two forks.

**3** Skim fat from the surface of the vegetable mixture. Blend or process vegetable mixture until smooth. Return chicken to the pan with the coconut milk; stir to combine. Ladle soup into serving bowls; sprinkle with coriander to serve, and drizzle with extra coconut milk, if you like.

**prep + cook time** 8 hours 30 minutes
**serves** 4 (3.5-litre cooker) or 2 (1.5-litre cooker)
**freezing** Suitable to freeze at the end of step 3.

# Cock-a-leekie soup

**for a 3.5-litre cooker:**
1.2kg whole chicken
2 cloves garlic, sliced thinly
4 medium leeks (1.4kg), sliced thinly
2 stalks celery (300g), trimmed, sliced thinly
4 sprigs fresh thyme
large pinch cayenne pepper
2½ litres chicken stock
170g pitted prunes
2 tablespoons coarsely chopped fresh oregano
2 tablespoons coarsely chopped fresh flat-leaf parsley

**for a 1.5-litre cooker:**
2 chicken legs (300g)
1 clove garlic, sliced thinly
2 small leeks (350g), sliced thinly
1 small stalk celery (75g), trimmed, sliced thinly
1 sprig fresh thyme
pinch cayenne pepper
625ml chicken stock
45g pitted prunes
1 tablespoon coarsely chopped fresh oregano
1 tablespoon coarsely chopped fresh flat-leaf parsley

**method:**
**1** Place chicken, garlic, leek, celery, thyme, cayenne pepper and 2 litres (3.5-litre cooker) or 500ml (1.5-litre cooker) of the stock in a slow cooker. Cook, covered, on low, for 8 hours.
**2** Carefully remove chicken from the cooker; when cool enough to handle, discard the skin and bones. Shred meat coarsely using two forks.
**3** Return chicken to cooker with prunes and remaining stock. Cook, covered, on high, for 30 minutes or until prunes soften and stock is hot. Discard thyme; season to taste.
**4** Stir oregano and parsley into soup to serve.

**prep + cook time** 9 hours
**serves** 6 (3.5-litre cooker) or 2 (1.5-litre cooker)
**freezing** Suitable to freeze at the end of step 3.

# Chicken & mushroom soup

**for a 3.5-litre cooker:**

1.2kg whole chicken
1 medium brown onion (150g) chopped coarsely
2 cloves garlic, crushed
300g chestnut mushrooms, halved
300g button mushrooms, halved
10g dried porcini mushrooms
1 stalk celery (150g), trimmed, chopped coarsely
2 medium potatoes (400g), chopped coarsely
1 litre water
500ml chicken stock
300ml single cream
4 tablespoons fresh chervil leaves

**for a 1.5-litre cooker:**

2 chicken legs (400g)
1 small brown onion (50g) chopped coarsely
1 clove garlic, crushed
100g chestnut mushrooms, halved
100g button mushrooms, halved
5g dried porcini mushrooms
½ stalk celery (50g), trimmed, chopped coarsely
1 medium potato (135g), chopped coarsely
330ml water
165ml chicken stock
100ml single cream
2 tablespoons fresh chervil leaves

**method:**

**1** Trim excess fat from chicken; place chicken in a slow cooker. Add onion, garlic, fresh and dried mushrooms, celery, potato, the water and stock. Cook, covered, on low, for 8 hours.

**2** Carefully remove chicken from the cooker; when cool enough to handle, discard the skin and bones. Shred the chicken meat coarsely using two forks.

**3** Using a stick blender, blend soup in cooker until smooth; stir in cream and shredded chicken meat. Cook, covered, on high, for 10 minutes or until hot. Season to taste. Serve soup sprinkled with chervil and drizzle with a little extra cream, if you like.

**prep + cook time** 8 hours 30 minutes
**serves** 4 (3.5-litre cooker) or 2 (1.5-litre cooker)
**freezing** Not suitable to freeze.

# Ham & lentil soup with gremolata

**for a 3.5-litre cooker:**
1.8kg ham hocks
100g puy lentils
1 tablespoon vegetable oil
2 medium brown onions (300g), chopped finely
2 medium carrots (240g), chopped finely
2 stalks celery (300g), trimmed, chopped finely
1 teaspoon fresh thyme leaves
500ml chicken stock
1.5 litres water

**gremolata**
2 cloves garlic, crushed
3 tablespoons finely chopped fresh flat-leaf parsley
2 teaspoons finely grated lemon rind

**for a 1.5-litre cooker:**
450g ham hocks
25g puy lentils
1 teaspoon vegetable oil
1 small brown onion (75g), chopped finely
1 small carrot (60g), chopped finely
1 small stalk celery (75g), trimmed, chopped finely
½ teaspoon fresh thyme leaves
125ml chicken stock
225ml water

**gremolata**
1 clove garlic, crushed
1 tablespoon finely chopped fresh flat-leaf parsley
1 teaspoon finely grated lemon rind

**method:**
**1** Rinse ham hocks. Place in a slow cooker.
**2** Rinse lentils; drain well.
**3** Heat oil in a medium frying pan over medium heat; cook onion, stirring, for 5 minutes or until softened. Transfer onion to the cooker with carrot, celery, thyme, lentils, stock and the water.
**4** Cook, covered, on low, for 8 hours. Carefully remove hocks from cooker. When cool enough to handle, remove and discard skin and bones. Shred meat finely using two forks. Return meat to cooker. Season to taste.
**5** When almost ready to serve, make gremolata; sprinkle over soup to serve.

**gremolata** Combine ingredients in a small bowl.

**prep + cook time** 8 hours 30 minutes
**serves** 6 (3.5-litre cooker) or 2 (1.5-litre cooker)
**freezing** Suitable to freeze at the end of step 4.
**tip** Make sure the ham hocks are not too large to fit in the slow cooker. Ask the butcher to cut them for you, if necessary.

# Beef & vegetable soup

**for a 3.5-litre cooker:**

1kg stewing steak, trimmed, cut into 2.5cm pieces
1 clove garlic, crushed
1 medium brown onion (150g), cut into 1cm pieces
2 stalks celery (300g), trimmed, cut into 1cm pieces
2 medium carrots (240g), cut into 1cm pieces
2 medium potatoes (400g), cut into 1cm pieces
400g canned chopped tomatoes
1 litre water
500ml beef stock
2 dried bay leaves
120g frozen peas
4 tablespoons coarsely chopped fresh flat-leaf parsley

**for a 1.5-litre cooker:**

330g stewing steak, trimmed, cut into 2.5cm pieces
1 small clove garlic, crushed
1 small brown onion (50g), cut into 1cm pieces
1 stalk celery (100g), trimmed, cut into 1cm pieces
1 medium carrot (80g), cut into 1cm pieces
1 medium potatoes (135g), cut into 1cm pieces
135g canned chopped tomatoes
330ml water
165ml beef stock
1 dried bay leaf
40g frozen peas
2 tablespoons coarsely chopped fresh flat-leaf parsley

**method:**

**1** Combine beef, garlic, onion, celery, carrot, potato, tomatoes, the water, stock and bay leaves in a slow cooker. Cook, covered, on low, for 9 hours.

**2** Add peas to cooker; cook, covered, for a further 30 minutes.

**3** Discard bay leaves. Season to taste. Serve soup sprinkled with parsley.

**prep + cook time** 9 hours 45 minutes
**serves** 4 (3.5-litre cooker) or 2 (1.5-litre cooker)
**freezing** Suitable to freeze.

# Lamb shank, fennel & vegetable soup

**for a 3.5-litre cooker:**
1 tablespoon olive oil
4 french-trimmed lamb shanks (1kg)
1 medium brown onion (150g), chopped coarsely
2 baby fennel bulbs (260g), sliced thinly
2 medium carrots (240g), chopped coarsely
4 cloves garlic, crushed
2 fresh small red chillies, chopped finely
2 teaspoons ground cumin
2 teaspoons ground coriander
1 teaspoon ground cinnamon
1 teaspoon caraway seeds
pinch saffron threads
1.5 litres water
500ml beef stock
400g canned chopped tomatoes
400g canned chickpeas, rinsed, drained
90g frozen petit pois
large handful fresh coriander leaves

**for a 1.5-litre cooker:**
1 teaspoon olive oil
1 french-trimmed lamb shank (250g)
1 small brown onion (35g), chopped coarsely
1 baby fennel bulb (65g), sliced thinly
1 medium carrot (60g), chopped coarsely
2 cloves garlic, crushed
½ fresh small red chilli, chopped finely
1 teaspoon ground cumin
1 teaspoon ground coriander
½ teaspoon ground cinnamon
½ teaspoon caraway seeds
pinch saffron threads
375ml water
125ml beef stock
100g canned chopped tomatoes
100g canned chickpeas, rinsed, drained
25g frozen petit pois
2 tablespoons fresh coriander leaves

**method:**
**1** Heat half the oil in large frying pan; cook lamb, until browned all over, then place in a slow cooker.
**2** Heat remaining oil in same pan; cook onion, fennel, carrot, garlic and chilli, stirring, until onion softens. Add spices; cook, stirring, until fragrant. Place vegetable mixture in cooker. Stir in the water, stock, undrained tomatoes and chickpeas. Cook, covered, on low, 10 hours.
**3** Remove lamb from cooker. When cool enough to handle, remove meat from bones, shred meat using two forks; discard bones. Stir meat, peas and coriander leaves into cooker. Heat for 10 minutes with the lid on. Season to taste.

**prep + cook time** 10 hours 30 minutes
**serves** 6 (3.5-litre cooker) or 2 (1.5-litre cooker)
**freezing** Suitable to freeze at the end of step 2.

# Vegetable harira

**for a 3.5-litre cooker:**

- 2 teaspoons each ground cumin, coriander and sweet smoked paprika
- 1 teaspoon each ground ginger, cinnamon and dried chilli flakes
- ¼ teaspoon ground nutmeg
- 1 large brown onion (200g), chopped finely
- 2 medium carrots (240g), chopped finely
- 4 stalks celery (600g), trimmed, chopped finely
- 5 medium tomatoes (750g), chopped finely
- 6 cloves garlic, crushed
- 2 tablespoons tomato paste
- 1.5 litres vegetable stock
- 1 litre water
- 200g puy lentils
- 400g canned chickpeas, rinsed, drained
- 4 tablespoons each finely chopped fresh flat-leaf parsley and coriander

**for a 1.5-litre cooker:**

- 1 teaspoon each ground cumin, coriander and sweet smoked paprika
- ½ teaspoon each ground ginger, cinnamon and dried chilli flakes
- pinch ground nutmeg
- 1 small brown onion (50g), chopped finely
- 1 small carrot (60g), chopped finely
- 1½ stalks celery (150g), trimmed, chopped finely
- 2 medium tomatoes (200g), chopped finely
- 2 cloves garlic, crushed
- 2 teaspoons tomato paste
- 375ml vegetable stock
- 250ml water
- 50g puy lentils
- 100g canned chickpeas, rinsed, drained
- 1 tablespoon each finely chopped fresh flat-leaf parsley and coriander

**method:**

**1** Dry-fry spices in a small frying pan over medium heat for 1 minute or until fragrant.

**2** Combine onion, carrot, celery, tomato, garlic, spices, paste, stock, the water and lentils in a slow cooker. Cook, covered, on low, for 8 hours. Season to taste.

**3** Add chickpeas to cooker and stir until heated through. Stir in parsley and coriander to serve.

**prep + cook time** 8 hours 45 minutes
**serves** 8 (3.5-litre cooker) or 2 (1.5-litre cooker)
**freezing** Not suitable to freeze.
**tip** Harira is a traditional soup that's eaten to break the fast of Ramadan. This is our vegetarian version, but lamb, chicken or beef can be added.

# Smoky chickpea & tomato soup

**for a 3.5-litre cooker:**
1.5kg tomatoes, quartered
1 large brown onion (200g), chopped coarsely
3 cloves garlic, chopped coarsely
1 stick celery (150g), trimmed, sliced thickly
1.2kg canned chickpeas, drained, rinsed
430ml chicken stock
2 teaspoons smoked paprika
1 tablespoon caster sugar
80g soured cream

**for a 1.5-litre cooker:**
375g tomatoes, quartered
1 small brown onion (50g), chopped coarsely
1 clove garlic, chopped coarsely
½ stick celery (40g), trimmed, sliced thickly
340g canned chickpeas, drained, rinsed
110ml chicken stock
1 teaspoon smoked paprika
1 teaspoon caster sugar
20g soured cream

**method:**
**1** Place tomato, onion, garlic, celery, chickpeas, stock, paprika and sugar in a slow cooker. Cook, covered, on low, for 8 hours.
**2** Using a slotted spoon, transfer 2 cups (3.5-litre cooker) or 2 tablespoons (1.5-litre cooker) of chickpeas to a medium bowl and reserve. Stand remaining soup 10 minutes, then process soup until smooth. Stir in reserved chickpeas. Season to taste.
**3** Serve soup topped with soured cream.

**prep + cook time** 8 hours 30 minutes
**serves** 6 (3.5-litre cooker) or 2 (1.5-litre cooker)
**freezing** Can be frozen at the end of step 2.
**tip** Choose the ripest tomatoes you can get. If you don't like tomato skins, you can either peel the tomatoes before adding to the cooker or strain the puréed soup before adding the reserved chickpeas.

# Spiced carrot & sweet potato soup

**for a 3.5-litre cooker:**
2 medium brown onions (300g), chopped coarsely
5 medium carrots (600g), chopped coarsely
3 small sweet potatoes (750g), chopped coarsely
1 tablespoon ground coriander
2 teaspoons cumin seeds
½ teaspoon dried chilli flakes
1 litre chicken stock
500ml water
200g Greek-style yoghurt
6 tablespoons fresh coriander sprigs

**for a 1.5-litre cooker:**
1 medium brown onion (100g), chopped coarsely
2 medium carrots (200g), chopped coarsely
1 small sweet potato (250g), chopped coarsely
2 teaspoons ground coriander
1 teaspoon cumin seeds
pinch dried chilli flakes
330ml chicken stock
165ml water
65g Greek-style yoghurt
2 tablespoons fresh coriander sprigs

**method:**
**1** Place onion, carrot, sweet potato, ground coriander, cumin, chilli, stock and the water in a slow cooker. Cook, covered, on low, for 8 hours.
**2** Cool soup 10 minutes. Blend or process soup, in batches, until smooth. Return soup to cooker. Cook, covered, on high, for 20 minutes or until hot. Season to taste.
**3** To serve, drizzle soup with yogurt and sprinkle with fresh coriander.

**prep + cook time** 9 hours
**serves** 4 (3.5-litre cooker) or 2 (1.5-litre cooker)
**freezing** Suitable to freeze.
**tip** If the soup is a little thick add a little more stock or water.

# Poultry & Pork

# Honey-mustard chicken

**for a 3.5-litre cooker:**
2 tablespoons cornflour
2 teaspoons dry mustard powder
125ml dry white wine
250ml chicken stock
70g wholegrain mustard
2 tablespoons honey
8 chicken thighs (1.6kg)
1 medium leek (350g), trimmed, sliced thickly
2 stalks celery (300g), trimmed, sliced thickly
400g baby carrots, peeled
120g frozen peas
80ml single cream
3 tablespoons coarsely chopped fresh flat-leaf parsley

**for a 1.5-litre cooker:**
3 teaspoons cornflour
1 teaspoon dry mustard powder
45ml dry white wine
85ml chicken stock
25g wholegrain mustard
3 teaspoons honey
4 small chicken thighs (540g)
1 small leek (120g), trimmed, sliced thickly
1 stalk celery (100g), trimmed, sliced thickly
135g baby carrots, peeled
40g frozen peas
30ml pouring cream
1 tablespoon coarsely chopped fresh flat-leaf parsley

**method:**

**1** Place cornflour and mustard powder in a slow cooker. Gradually whisk in wine and stock until smooth. Add mustard and honey; whisk until smooth.

**2** Remove and discard fat and skin from chicken. Place chicken, leek, celery and carrots in cooker. Cook, covered, on low, for 6 hours.

**3** Add peas to cooker; cook, covered, for 20 minutes. Stir in cream; season to taste. Sprinkle chicken with parsley to serve.

**prep + cook time** 6 hours 45 minutes
**serves** 4 (3.5-litre cooker) or 2 (1.5-litre cooker)
**freezing** Not suitable to freeze.

# Butter chicken

**for a 3.5-litre cooker:**

- 12 chicken thighs (2.4kg), skin removed
- 2 tablespoons lemon juice
- 1 teaspoon chilli powder
- 210g Greek-style yoghurt
- 5cm piece fresh ginger (25g), grated
- 2 teaspoons garam masala
- 45g butter
- 1 tablespoon vegetable oil
- 1 medium brown onion (150g), chopped finely
- 4 cloves garlic, crushed
- 1 teaspoon ground coriander
- 1 teaspoon ground cumin
- 1 teaspoon sweet paprika
- 2 tablespoons tomato paste
- 410g tomato purée
- 160ml chicken stock
- 2 tablespoons honey
- 1 cinnamon stick
- 80ml single cream
- 80g ricotta cheese
- 6 tablespoons fresh coriander leaves

**for a 1.5-litre cooker:**

- 4 chicken thighs (800g), skin removed
- 3 teaspoons lemon juice
- ½ teaspoon chilli powder
- 70g Greek-style yoghurt
- 2cm piece fresh ginger (10g), grated
- 1 teaspoon garam masala
- 15g butter
- 2 teaspoons vegetable oil
- 1 small brown onion (50g), chopped finely
- 2 cloves garlic, crushed
- ½ teaspoon ground coriander
- ½ teaspoon ground cumin
- 1 teaspoon sweet paprika
- 3 teaspoons tomato paste
- 140g tomato purée
- 55ml chicken stock
- 3 teaspoons honey
- ½ cinnamon stick
- 30ml single cream
- 30g ricotta cheese
- 2 tablespoons fresh coriander leaves

**method:**

**1** Combine chicken, juice and chilli powder in a large bowl. Cover; refrigerate 30 minutes.

**2** Stir yoghurt, ginger and half the garam masala into chicken mixture.

**3** Heat butter and oil in a large frying pan; cook chicken, in batches, until browned all over. Transfer to a slow cooker.

**4** Cook onion and garlic in same pan, stirring, until onion softens. Add ground spices, paprika and remaining garam masala; cook, stirring, until fragrant. Remove from heat; stir in tomato paste, purée, stock, honey and cinnamon stick. Transfer to slow cooker. Cook, covered, on low, 4 hours.

**5** Stir in cream; season to taste.

**6** Serve topped with ricotta and coriander leaves.

**prep + cook time** 4 hours 30 minutes + refrigeration time
**serves** 6 (3.5-litre cooker) or 2 (1.5-litre cooker)
**freezing** Suitable to freeze at the end of step 4.

# Spicy tomato & saffron chicken casserole

**for a 3.5-litre cooker:**
35g plain flour
2 tablespoons moroccan seasoning
6 chicken thighs (1.2kg)
1 tablespoon vegetable oil
1 large brown onion (200g), sliced thickly
2 cloves garlic, crushed
2.5cm piece fresh ginger (15g), grated
1 fresh red chilli, sliced thinly
500ml chicken stock
400g canned chopped tomatoes
70g tomato paste
¼ teaspoon saffron threads

**preserved lemon gremolata**
4 tablespoons finely chopped fresh flat-leaf parsley
1 tablespoon thinly sliced preserved lemon rind
1 clove garlic, crushed

for a 1.5-litre cooker:
1 tablespoon plain flour
3 teaspoons moroccan seasoning
2 chicken thighs (400g)
2 teaspoons vegetable oil
1 small brown onion (65g), sliced thickly
1 clove garlic, crushed
1cm piece fresh ginger (5g), grated
1 fresh small red chilli, sliced thinly
165ml chicken stock
135g canned chopped tomatoes
25g tomato paste
pinch saffron threads

**preserved lemon gremolata**
2 tablespoons finely chopped fresh flat-leaf parsley
2 teaspoons thinly sliced preserved lemon rind
1 small clove garlic, crushed

**method:**
**1** Combine flour and half the seasoning in small shallow bowl; toss chicken in flour mixture to coat, shake off excess. Heat half the oil in a large frying pan; cook chicken, in batches, until browned. Transfer to a slow cooker.
**2** Heat remaining oil in same pan, add onion, garlic, ginger, chilli and remaining seasoning; cook, stirring, until onion softens. Add a quarter of the stock; cook, stirring, until mixture boils.
**3** Stir onion mixture into cooker with remaining stock, undrained tomatoes, paste and saffron. Cook, covered, on low, 6 hours. Season to taste.
**4** Just before serving make the preserved lemon gremolata. Sprinkle over casserole.

**preserved lemon gremolata**
Combine ingredients in small bowl.

**prep + cook time** 6 hours 30 minutes
**serves** 6 (3.5-litre cooker) or 2 (1.5-litre cooker)
**freezing** Suitable to freeze at the end of step 3.

# Turkey with bacon, celery & sage seasoning

**for a 3.5-litre cooker:**
2 medium brown onions (300g)
2.2kg turkey legs
2 teaspoons vegetable oil
60g butter
1 clove garlic, chopped finely
4 rindless middle bacon slices (175g), chopped finely
1 stalk celery (150g), trimmed, chopped finely
140g stale breadcrumbs
1 egg
1 tablespoon chopped fresh sage
125ml water
2 tablespoons plain flour
160g cranberry sauce

**for a 1.5-litre cooker:**
1 medium brown onion (100g)
750g turkey leg
2 teaspoons vegetable oil
20g butter
1 small clove garlic, chopped finely
2 rindless middle bacon slices (60g), chopped finely
½ stalk celery (50g), trimmed, chopped finely
50g stale breadcrumbs
1 small egg
2 teaspoons chopped fresh sage
45ml water
3 teaspoons plain flour
55g cranberry sauce

**method:**

**1** Cut half the onion quantity into wedges and place in a slow cooker. Finely chop remaining onion; reserve.

**2** Cut through the thigh joint between turkey drumstick and thigh to separate. If necessary, cut the leg to fit the 1.5-litre cooker, or ask your butcher to do this for you. Season.

**3** Heat oil in a large frying pan over medium heat; cook drumstick and thigh, one piece at a time, until browned. Transfer to the slow cooker; placing the thigh on the base and the drumstick on top.

**4** Melt one third of the butter in the same frying pan over medium heat. Add chopped onion, garlic, bacon and celery; cook, stirring, until bacon is browned. Transfer to a large bowl; cool slightly. Add breadcrumbs, egg and sage; stir to combine.

**5** Grease two 30cm x 40cm pieces of foil (for 1.5-litre cooker use only one piece of foil and make one parcel). Divide bacon mixture evenly between foil sheets; shape each into a 20cm log. Roll up to enclose. Place foil parcels around turkey.

**6** Cook, covered, on low, for 8 hours. Remove foil parcels and turkey from the cooker. Cover to keep warm.

**7** Strain cooking liquid into a medium heatproof jug; reserve onion. Skim fat from surface. Add enough of the water to make 625ml of liquid for a 3.5-litre cooker or 210ml of liquid for a 1.5-litre cooker.

**8** Melt remaining butter in a medium saucepan over medium heat; cook the reserved onion, stirring, until browned. Add flour; cook, stirring, until mixture thickens and bubbles. Gradually add cooking liquid; stir until mixture boils and thickens.

**9** Slice turkey; serve with gravy, seasoning and cranberry sauce.

**prep + cook time** 9 hours 30 minutes
**serves** 6 (3.5-litre cooker) or 2 (1.5-litre cooker)
**freezing** Not suitable to freeze.
**tip** You can serve the turkey with the strained and seasoned juices instead of making the gravy.

# Pork & veal meatballs

**for a 3.5-litre cooker:**
1kg minced pork and veal
70g stale breadcrumbs
120g finely grated cheddar cheese
2 eggs
large handful finely chopped fresh flat-leaf parsley
4 cloves garlic, crushed
900g passata sauce
1 medium fennel bulb (300g), trimmed, sliced thinly
2 medium brown onions (300g), chopped finely
80g flaked parmesan cheese

**for a 1.5-litre cooker:**
330g minced pork and veal
25g stale breadcrumbs
40g finely grated cheddar cheese
1 egg
3 tablespoons finely chopped fresh flat-leaf parsley
2 cloves garlic, crushed
300g passata sauce
1 small fennel bulb (100g), trimmed, sliced thinly
1 medium brown onion (100g), chopped finely
30g flaked parmesan cheese

**method:**
**1** Combine mince, breadcrumbs, cheddar, eggs, parsley and half the garlic in large bowl, season. Roll rounded tablespoons of mixture into balls. Place on tray, cover; refrigerate 20 minutes.
**2** Combine sauce, fennel, onion and remaining garlic in a slow cooker; add meatballs. Cook, covered, on high, 3½ hours. Season to taste.
**3** Serve sprinkled with parmesan.

**prep + cook time** 4 hours + refrigeration
**serves** 6 (3.5-litre cooker) or 2–3 (1.5-litre cooker)
**freezing** Suitable to freeze at the end of step 2.

# Five-spice caramel pork belly

**for a 3.5-litre cooker:**
2kg boned pork belly, rind removed
2 litres water
250ml coconut water
250ml water, extra
180ml fish sauce
110g brown sugar
2 teaspoons five-spice powder
16 garlic cloves, unpeeled
6 eggs, at room temperature
6 fresh small red chillies
3 tablespoons fresh coriander sprigs

**caramel**
220g caster sugar
125ml water

**for a 1.5-litre cooker:**
675g boned pork belly, rind removed
670ml water
85ml coconut water
85ml water, extra
60ml fish sauce
40g brown sugar
1 teaspoon five-spice powder
6 garlic cloves, unpeeled
2 eggs, at room temperature
2 fresh small red chillies
1 tablespoon fresh coriander sprigs

**caramel**
75g caster sugar
45ml water

**prep + cook time** 7 hours
**serves** 6 (3.5-litre cooker) or 2–3 (1.5-litre cooker)
**freezing** Suitable to freeze at the end of step 4.
**tip** Coconut water is readily available in tetra packs and cans from a variety of supermarkets. Ensure it's labelled 100 per cent coconut water, and that it is not sweetened.

**method:**
**1** Cut pork into 4cm pieces.
**2** Place pork and the water in a large saucepan, bring to the boil over medium heat. Boil 5 minutes, skimming impurities from the surface; drain.
**3** Meanwhile, make caramel.
**4** Place pork in a slow cooker with caramel, coconut water, the water, sauce, sugar, five-spice and unpeeled garlic cloves. Cook, covered, on low, for 6 hours.
**5** Meanwhile, place eggs in a medium saucepan; cover with cold water. Bring to the boil; boil eggs 6 minutes. Transfer to a bowl of cold water and cool slightly before peeling.
**6** Add eggs and chillies to cooker. Cook, uncovered, on high, for 30 minutes; skim fat from surface. Sprinkle with coriander before serving.

**caramel** Combine sugar and the water in a small saucepan; stir over high heat, without boiling, until sugar dissolves. Bring to the boil. Boil, uncovered, without stirring, until a deep golden caramel.

# Smoky sticky pork ribs with coleslaw

**for a 3.5-litre cooker:**
2kg baby back pork ribs
3 cloves garlic, crushed
280g barbecue sauce
60ml lemon juice
55g brown sugar
2 teaspoons sweet smoked paprika
1 teaspoon Tabasco sauce

**cheesy coleslaw**
¼ small green cabbage (300g)
¼ small red cabbage (300g)
1 large carrot (180g)
½ small red onion (50g)
120g coarsely grated vintage cheddar cheese
2 tablespoons coarsely chopped fresh chives
225g mayonnaise
60ml cider vinegar

**for a 1.5-litre cooker:**
675g baby back pork ribs
1 clove garlic, crushed
95g barbecue sauce
20ml lemon juice
20g brown sugar
1 teaspoon sweet smoked paprika
½ teaspoon Tabasco sauce

**cheesy coleslaw**
100g green cabbage
100g red cabbage
1 medium carrot (60g)
¼ small red onion (20g)
40g coarsely grated vintage cheddar cheese
1 tablespoon coarsely chopped fresh chives
75g mayonnaise
20ml cider vinegar

**prep + cook time** 4 hours 45 minutes
**serves** 4 (3.5-litre cooker) or 2 (1.5-litre cooker)
**freezing** Not suitable to freeze.

**method:**
**1** Cut pork ribs into pieces that will fit into the slow cooker. or ask your butcher to do this for you
**2** Combine garlic and remaining ingredients in a large shallow dish; add pork, turn to coat pork in the marinade. Transfer pork and marinade to a slow cooker. Cook, covered, on high, for 4 hours. Turn ribs once during cooking time for even cooking.
**3** When almost ready to serve, make the cheesy coleslaw.
**4** Carefully remove ribs from the cooker; cover to keep warm. Transfer sauce to a medium frying pan; bring to the boil. Reduce heat; simmer, uncovered, skimming fat from surface, for about 10 minutes or until sauce has reduced to 250ml for a 3.5-litre slow cooker or 85ml for a 1.5-litre slow cooker.
**5** Drizzle pork with sauce. Serve with coleslaw.

**cheesy coleslaw** Finely shred cabbages. Coarsely grate carrot and thinly slice the onion. Combine the cheese, chives, mayonnaise, vinegar and vegetables in a bowl; toss gently to combine. Season to taste.

# Pork vindaloo

**for a 3.5-litre cooker:**
1.2kg pork neck fillet
2 large brown onions (400g), sliced thinly
5cm piece fresh ginger (25g), grated
2 cloves garlic, grated
400g canned chopped tomatoes
150g vindaloo paste
2 tablespoons tomato paste
180ml beef stock
handful fresh coriander leaves

**for a 1.5-litre cooker:**
400g pork neck fillet
1 medium brown onion (135g), sliced thinly
2cm piece fresh ginger (10g), grated
1 clove garlic, grated
135g canned chopped tomatoes
50g vindaloo paste
1 tablespoon tomato paste
60ml beef stock
2 tablespoons fresh coriander leaves

**method:**

**1** Cut pork into 3cm pieces; discard any excess fat.

**2** Place pork, onion, ginger, garlic, tomatoes, the vindaloo and tomato pastes, and stock in a slow cooker. Cook, covered, on low, for 8 hours. Sprinkle with coriander to serve.

**prep + cook time** 8 hours 30 minutes
**serves** 6 (3.5-litre cooker) or 2–3 (1.5-litre cooker)
**freezing** Suitable to freeze without coriander.

# Sweet & sour Italian pork with peppers

**for a 3.5-litre cooker:**

1.5kg piece pork neck fillet
2 tablespoons olive oil
2 medium red peppers (400g)
2 medium brown onions (300g) chopped finely
1 stalk celery (150g), trimmed, chopped coarsely
2 cloves garlic, chopped finely
55g caster sugar
125ml red wine vinegar
2 tablespoons tomato paste
125ml chicken stock
40g sultanas
2 tablespoons pine nuts
2 tablespoons chopped fresh flat-leaf parsley

**for a 1.5-litre cooker:**

400–500g piece pork neck fillet
3 teaspoons olive oil
1 medium red pepper (135g)
1 medium brown onion (100g) chopped finely
½ stalk celery (50g), trimmed, chopped coarsely
1 clove garlic, chopped finely
20g caster sugar
45ml red wine vinegar
3 teaspoons tomato paste
45ml chicken stock
15g sultanas
3 teaspoons pine nuts
1 tablespoon chopped fresh flat-leaf parsley

**method:**

**1** Tie the pork with kitchen string at 2cm intervals. Make sure it will fit in your cooker and cut to fit if necessary. Heat half the oil in a large frying pan over medium-high heat; cook the pork until browned. Transfer to a slow cooker.

**2** Meanwhile, cut peppers lengthways into eighths; discard seeds and membranes.

**3** Heat remaining oil in same pan over medium heat; cook onion, celery and garlic, stirring occasionally, for 5 minutes or until softened. Add sugar; cook, stirring occasionally, about 10 minutes or until golden and caramelised. Add vinegar to the pan; bring to the boil. Stir in paste and stock; bring to the boil, then pour over pork. Add sultanas and pepper to the cooker.

**4** Cook, covered, on low, for 8 hours. Carefully remove pork from cooker; transfer to serving plate, cover to keep warm.

**5** Meanwhile, toast nuts in a dry frying pan, stirring continuously over medium heat until just golden. Remove immediately from pan. Spoon sauce over pork and sprinkle with nuts and parsley.

**prep + cook time** 8 hours 45 minutes
**serves** 6 (3.5-litre cooker) or 2–3 (1.5-litre cooker)
**freezing** Suitable to freeze at the end of step 4.

# Chorizo, chilli & bean stew

**for a 3.5-litre cooker:**

- 1 tablespoon olive oil
- 1 large red onion (300g), chopped coarsely
- 3 chorizo sausages (500g), chopped coarsely
- 4 cloves garlic, crushed
- 1 teaspoon dried chilli flakes
- 1 medium red pepper (200g), chopped coarsely
- 150g fine green beans, halved
- 800g canned cannellini beans, rinsed, drained
- 800g canned chopped tomatoes
- 80ml chicken stock
- 2 bay leaves
- 4 tablespoons coarsely chopped fresh flat-leaf parsley

**for a 1.5-litre cooker:**

- 2 teaspoons olive oil
- 1 medium red onion (100g), chopped coarsely
- 1 chorizo sausage (165g), chopped coarsely
- 2 cloves garlic, crushed
- ½ teaspoon dried chilli flakes
- ½ medium red pepper (65g), chopped coarsely
- 50g fine green beans, halved
- 270g canned cannellini beans, rinsed, drained
- 270g canned chopped tomatoes
- 30ml chicken stock
- 1 bay leaf
- 2 tablespoons coarsely chopped fresh flat-leaf parsley

**method:**

**1** Heat oil in large frying pan; cook onion and chorizo, stirring, until browned lightly. Add garlic and chilli flakes; cook, stirring, until fragrant.

**2** Combine pepper, both beans, tomatoes, stock, bay leaves and chorizo mixture in a slow cooker. Cook, covered, on low, 3 hours.

**3** Discard bay leaves. Season to taste; sprinkle with parsley.

**prep + cook time** 3 hours 30 minutes

**serves** 6 (3.5-litre cooker) or 2–3 (1.5-litre cooker)

**freezing** Suitable to freeze at the end of step 2.

# Beef

# Moroccan beef meatballs

**for a 3.5-litre cooker:**
2 slices white bread (90g)
125ml milk
1kg minced beef
2 tablespoons finely chopped fresh coriander stems
1 tablespoon ground cumin
1 tablespoon ground coriander
1 tablespoon sweet paprika
2 teaspoons ground ginger
1 teaspoon ground cinnamon
1 large brown onion (200g), chopped finely
4 cloves garlic, chopped finely
1 egg, beaten
1 tablespoon olive oil
2 tablespoons tomato paste
700g passata
125ml beef stock
2 tablespoons honey
6 tablespoons fresh coriander leaves

**for a 1.5-litre cooker:**
1 slice white bread (30g)
45ml milk
330g minced beef
1 tablespoon finely chopped fresh coriander stems
2 teaspoons ground cumin
2 teaspoons ground coriander
2 teaspoons sweet paprika
1 teaspoon ground ginger
½ teaspoon ground cinnamon
1 medium brown onion (65g), chopped finely
2 cloves garlic, chopped finely
1 small egg, beaten
2 teaspoons olive oil
2 teaspoons tomato paste
240g passata
45ml beef stock
2 teaspoons honey
3 tablespoons fresh coriander leaves

**method:**
**1** Remove and discard crusts from bread. Combine bread and milk in a small bowl; stand for 10 minutes.
**2** Combine bread mixture, beef, coriander stems, cumin, ground coriander, paprika, ginger, cinnamon, and half of the onion and garlic, in a large bowl with enough of the egg to bind. Roll level tablespoons of mixture into balls, place in a slow cooker.
**3** Heat oil in a large frying pan over medium heat. Cook the remaining onion and garlic, stirring, for 5 minutes or until onion softens. Stir in paste, passata, stock and honey; transfer to slow cooker. Cook, covered, on low, for 6 hours. Season to taste. Sprinkle with fresh coriander to serve.

**prep + cook time** 6 hours 45 minutes
**serves** 6 (3.5-litre cooker) or 2–3 (1.5-litre cooker)
**freezing** Suitable to freeze at the end of step 3 without coriander.

# Tuscan beef stew

**for a 3.5-litre cooker:**
6 pieces beef osso buco (1.2kg)
1 tablespoon olive oil
1 large brown onion (200g), chopped coarsely
3 cloves garlic, crushed
6 anchovy fillets, drained, chopped finely
2 tablespoons plain flour
60ml balsamic vinegar
2 tablespoons tomato paste
400g canned chopped tomatoes
250ml beef stock
60ml water
4 sprigs fresh rosemary
120g pitted green olives

**for a 1.5-litre cooker:**
2 pieces beef osso buco (400g)
2 teaspoons olive oil
1 medium brown onion (65g), chopped coarsely
1 clove garlic, crushed
2 anchovy fillets, drained, chopped finely
3 teaspoons plain flour
20ml balsamic vinegar
3 teaspoons tomato paste
135g canned chopped tomatoes
85ml beef stock
20ml water
2 sprigs fresh rosemary
40g pitted green olives

**method:**

**1** Trim excess fat from the beef. Heat oil in a large frying pan over medium-high heat. Cook beef, in batches, until browned. Transfer to a slow cooker.

**2** Add onion, garlic and anchovy to same pan; cook, stirring, 1 minute or until fragrant. Add flour; cook, stirring, 1 minute. Stir in vinegar and paste, then tomatoes, stock, the water and rosemary. Transfer mixture to slow cooker.

**3** Cook, covered, on low, 6 hours. Season to taste. Just before serving, stir in olives.

**prep + cook time** 6 hours 30 minutes
**serves** 6 (3.5-litre cooker) or 2–3 (1.5-litre cooker)
**freezing** Suitable to freeze at the end of step 3.

# Beer & thyme beef cheeks

**for a 3.5-litre cooker:**
16 baby onions (400g)
3 stalks celery (450g), trimmed, chopped coarsely
400g baby carrots, trimmed
4 sprigs fresh thyme
375ml beer
250ml beef stock
70g tomato paste
2 tablespoons worcestershire sauce
1 tablespoon brown sugar
1 tablespoon wholegrain mustard
2kg trimmed beef cheeks
150g green beans, trimmed

**for a 1.5-litre cooker:**
4 baby onions (100g)
1 stalk celery (100g), trimmed, chopped coarsely
100g baby carrots, trimmed
1 sprig fresh thyme
100ml beer
60ml beef stock
20g tomato paste
2 teaspoons worcestershire sauce
1 teaspoon brown sugar
1 teaspoon wholegrain mustard
500g trimmed beef cheeks
50g green beans, trimmed

**method:**

**1** Peel onions, leaving root end intact. Combine onions with celery, carrots, thyme, beer, stock, tomato paste, sauce, sugar and mustard in a slow cooker. Add beef; turn to coat in mixture. Cook, covered, on low, for 9 hours 30 minutes.

**2** Discard thyme. Add beans to cooker; cook, covered, on low, for 30 minutes. Season to taste. Serve beef sprinkled with extra fresh thyme.

**prep + cook time** 10 hours 30 minutes
**serves** 6 (3.5-litre cooker) or 2 (1.5-litre cooker)
**freezing** Suitable to freeze.

# Beef casserole with cheesy herb dumplings

**for a 3.5-litre cooker:**
1kg stewing steak
1 tablespoon olive oil
1 large brown onion (200g), chopped coarsely
2 cloves garlic, crushed
2 tablespoons tomato paste
400g canned whole peeled tomatoes
250ml beef stock
125ml dry red wine
4 sprigs fresh thyme
250g button mushrooms, halved
150g self-raising flour
50g cold butter, chopped finely
2 tablespoons finely chopped fresh flat-leaf parsley
80g coarsely grated vintage cheddar cheese
125ml buttermilk, approximately

**for a 1.5-litre cooker:**
330g stewing steak
2 teaspoons olive oil
1 medium brown onion (65g), chopped coarsely
1 clove garlic, crushed
3 teaspoons tomato paste
135g canned whole peeled tomatoes
85ml beef stock
45ml dry red wine
2 sprigs fresh thyme
85g button mushrooms, halved
50g self-raising flour
20g cold butter, chopped finely
1 tablespoon finely chopped fresh flat-leaf parsley
30g coarsely grated vintage cheddar cheese
45ml buttermilk, approximately

**method:**

**1** Cut beef into 3cm pieces. Heat oil in a large frying pan over medium-high heat. Cook beef, in batches, until browned. Transfer to a slow cooker.

**2** Add onion and garlic to same pan; cook, stirring, 5 minutes or until onion softens. Add paste, tomatoes, stock, wine and thyme to pan; bring to the boil. Transfer mixture to slow cooker; add mushrooms.

**3** Cook, covered, on low, for 7 hours. Remove and discard thyme sprigs. Season to taste.

**4** Meanwhile, place flour in a medium bowl; rub in butter. Add half of the parsley and half of the cheese; stir to combine. Stir in enough buttermilk to make a soft, sticky dough. Drop rounded tablespoons of the dumpling mixture, 2cm apart, on top of the casserole; scatter with remaining cheese. Cook, covered, 1 hour or until dumplings are cooked through. Scatter with remaining parsley to serve.

**prep + cook time** 8 hours 30 minutes
**serves** 6 (3.5-litre cooker) or 2–3 (1.5-litre cooker)
**freezing** Suitable to freeze at the end of step 3.

# Coconut curried beef

**for a 3.5-litre cooker:**
1kg diced beef
2 tablespoons thai yellow curry paste
410ml coconut milk
500ml beef stock
4 teaspoons finely grated fresh ginger
3 cloves garlic, crushed
2 medium brown onions (300g), cut into thin wedges
2 fresh kaffir lime leaves
8 fresh curry leaves
2 tablespoons fish sauce
2 tablespoons grated palm sugar
150g mangetout
2 tablespoons finely chopped peanuts, toasted
3 tablespoons fresh thai basil leaves
1 fresh red chilli, sliced thinly

**for a 1.5-litre cooker:**
330g diced beef
3 teaspoons thai yellow curry paste
140ml coconut milk
165ml beef stock
1½ teaspoons finely grated fresh ginger
1 clove garlic, crushed
1 small brown onion (100g), cut into thin wedges
1 fresh kaffir lime leaf
3 fresh curry leaves
3 teaspoons fish sauce
3 teaspoons grated palm sugar
50g mangetout
3 teaspoons finely chopped peanuts, toasted
1 tablespoon fresh thai basil leaves
½ fresh red chilli, sliced thinly

**method:**
**1** Place beef, paste and coconut milk in a slow cooker; stir until paste dissolves.
**2** Add stock, ginger, garlic, onion, kaffir lime leaves, curry leaves, sauce and sugar to cooker. Cook, covered, on high, for 2 hours. Reduce to low; cook for a further 8 hours. Season to taste.
**3** Discard lime leaves. Stir in mangetout; cook, covered, on low, for 10 minutes or until mangetout are tender. Season to taste. Serve beef topped with peanuts, basil and chilli.

**prep + cook time** 10 hours 45 minutes
**serves** 4 (3.5-litre cooker) or 2 (1.5-litre cooker)
**freezing** Not suitable to freeze.
**tip** If you can't find Thai basil, you can substitute a mix of half fresh basil and half fresh mint instead.

# Beef rib bourguignon

**for a 3.5-litre cooker:**

12 shallots (300g)
200g button mushrooms
200g chestnut mushrooms
4 rindless bacon slices (260g), cut into 5cm lengths
3 cloves garlic, sliced thinly
2 fresh thyme sprigs
2 fresh bay leaves
375ml dry red wine
750ml beef stock
2 tablespoons tomato paste
1.2kg beef short ribs
6 tablespoons finely chopped fresh flat-leaf parsley

**for a 1.5-litre cooker:**

4 shallots (100g)
65g button mushrooms
65g chestnut mushrooms
2 rindless bacon slices (90g), cut into 5cm lengths
1 clove garlic, sliced thinly
1 fresh thyme sprig
1 fresh bay leaf
125ml dry red wine
250ml beef stock
3 teaspoons tomato paste
400g beef short ribs
2 tablespoons finely chopped fresh flat-leaf parsley

**method:**

**1** Place shallots, mushrooms, bacon, garlic, thyme, bay leaves, wine, stock, paste and beef in a slow cooker. Cook, covered, on low, for 8 hours. Season to taste.

**2** Discard thyme and bay leaves. Stir in half the parsley; season to taste. Serve topped with the remaining parsley.

**prep + cook time** 8 hours 30 minutes
**serves** 4 (3.5-litre cooker) or 2 (1.5-litre cooker)
**freezing** Not suitable to freeze.
**tip** Cut the shallots in half if they are large.

# Braised Asian-style beef ribs

**for a 3.5-litre cooker:**
2kg racks beef short ribs
190ml hoisin sauce
60ml reduced-salt soy sauce
60ml mirin
2 x 3cm strips orange rind
90g honey
5cm piece fresh ginger (25g), grated
3 cloves garlic, crushed
1 fresh red chilli, sliced thinly
2 teaspoons sesame oil

**for a 1.5-litre cooker:**
675g racks beef short ribs
65ml hoisin sauce
20ml reduced-salt soy sauce
20ml mirin
1 x 3cm strip orange rind
30g honey
2.5cm piece fresh ginger (10g), grated
1 clove garlic, crushed
½ fresh red chilli, sliced thinly
1 teaspoon sesame oil

**method:**

**1** Cut rib racks into pieces to fit into a slow cooker or ask your butcher to do this for you. Place ribs in cooker. Combine remaining ingredients in a large jug; pour sauce over ribs. Cook, covered, on low, 8 hours. Season to taste.

**2** Cut ribs into serving-sized pieces; serve with sauce.

**prep + cook time** 8 hours 30 minutes
**serves** 6 (3.5-litre cooker) or 2–3 (1.5-litre cooker)
**freezing** Not suitable to freeze.

# Hoisin & star anise oxtail

**for a 3.5-litre cooker:**
2kg oxtail, cut into 5cm pieces
160ml hoisin sauce
250ml beef stock
60ml dry sherry
1 tablespoon finely grated orange rind
80ml orange juice
3 cloves garlic, crushed
2 tablespoons brown sugar
½ teaspoon cracked black pepper
2 star anise
500g bok choy, trimmed, quartered lengthways
1 fresh red chilli, sliced thinly
3 spring onions, sliced thinly

**for a 1.5-litre cooker:**
675g oxtail, cut into 5cm pieces
55ml hoisin sauce
85ml beef stock
20ml dry sherry
2 teaspoons finely grated orange rind
30ml orange juice
1 clove garlic, crushed
3 teaspoons brown sugar
pinch cracked black pepper
1 star anise
165g bok choy, trimmed, quartered lengthways
½ fresh red chilli, sliced thinly
1 spring onion, sliced thinly

**method:**
**1** Trim excess fat from oxtail. Pack oxtail tightly, in a single layer, in the base of a slow cooker. Whisk sauce, stock, sherry, rind, juice, garlic, sugar and pepper in a medium jug until combined; add star anise. Pour mixture over oxtail in cooker. Cook, covered, on low, for 8 hours.
**2** Discard star anise. Remove oxtail; cover to keep warm. Skim fat from surface of liquid in cooker. Add bok choy to cooker; cook, uncovered, on high, for 5 minutes or until wilted.
**3** Return oxtail to cooker; cook, uncovered, on high, until oxtail is heated through. Season to taste. Serve oxtail with bok choy and cooking liquid. Sprinkle with chilli and sliced spring onions.

**prep + cook time** 9 hours 30 minutes
**serves** 4 (3.5-litre cooker) or 2 (1.5-litre cooker)
**freezing** Suitable to freeze.
**tip** To thicken the liquid, uncover the cooker for the last hour of cooking in step 1.

# Lamb

# Lamb, spinach & chickpea rice pilaf

**for a 3.5-litre cooker:**
1kg boned lamb shoulder
2 tablespoons olive oil
1 large brown onion (200g), sliced thinly
4 cloves garlic, crushed
1 tablespoon ground cumin
1 tablespoon ground coriander
2 teaspoons ground allspice
2 teaspoons chilli powder
750ml chicken stock
400g basmati rice
1 bunch swiss chard (1kg), trimmed, chopped coarsely
400g canned chickpeas, rinsed, drained
100g raisins
80g pine nuts, toasted
6 tablespoons coarsely chopped fresh coriander

for a 1.5-litre cooker:
250g boned lamb shoulder
1 tablespoon olive oil
1 small brown onion (50g), sliced thinly
1 clove garlic, crushed
1 teaspoon ground cumin
1 teaspoon ground coriander
½ teaspoon ground allspice
½ teaspoon chilli powder
200ml chicken stock
100g basmati rice
¼ bunch swiss chard (250g), trimmed, chopped coarsely
100g canned chickpeas, rinsed, drained
25g raisins
20g pine nuts, toasted
2 tablespoons coarsely chopped fresh coriander

**method:**
**1** Cut lamb into 2cm pieces. Heat half the oil in a large frying pan over medium heat; cook lamb, in batches, until browned. Transfer to a slow cooker.
**2** Heat remaining oil in the same pan; cook onion and garlic, stirring, for 5 minutes or until onion softens. Add spices; cook, stirring, for 1 minute or until fragrant. Stir in stock; bring to the boil. Transfer mixture to the slow cooker. Cook, covered, on low, for 7 hours.
**3** Stir in rice; top with swiss chard and chickpeas. Cook, covered, on high, for 50 minutes. Season to taste.
**4** Stir in raisins, pine nuts and coriander to serve.

**prep + cook time** 8 hours 30 minutes
**serves** 6 (3.5-litre cooker) or 2 (1.5-litre cooker)
**freezing** Suitable to freeze at the end of step 2.

# Lamb shank & spinach korma curry

**for a 3.5-litre cooker:**

6 french-trimmed lamb shanks (1.5kg)
400g canned chopped tomatoes
1 large brown onion (200g), sliced thickly
300ml single cream
100g baby spinach leaves
120g frozen peas

**korma paste**

1 tablespoon cumin seeds
3 cloves garlic, quartered
5cm piece fresh ginger (25g), grated finely
50g toasted cashew nuts
60ml tomato ketchup
3 tablespoons coarsely chopped coriander stems
2 tablespoons desiccated coconut
1 tablespoon garam masala
2 teaspoons ground coriander
2 teaspoons ground turmeric
2 teaspoons sea salt flakes
60ml vegetable oil

**for a 1.5-litre cooker:**

2 french-trimmed lamb shanks (500g)
135g canned chopped tomatoes
1 medium brown onion (65g), sliced thickly
100ml single cream
35g baby spinach leaves
40g frozen peas

**korma paste**

2 teaspoons cumin seeds
1 clove garlic, quartered
2.5cm piece fresh ginger (10g), grated finely
20g toasted cashew nuts
20ml tomato ketchup
1 tablespoon coarsely chopped coriander stems
3 teaspoons desiccated coconut
2 teaspoons garam masala
1 teaspoon ground coriander
1 teaspoon ground turmeric
1 teaspoon sea salt flakes
20ml vegetable oil

**method:**

**1** Make korma paste.
**2** Combine lamb, tomatoes, onion, cream and paste in a slow cooker. Cook, covered, on low, for 8 hours.
**3** Add spinach and peas to cooker; cook, covered, for 10 minutes or until heated through.

**korma paste** Place cumin seeds in a small frying pan; cook, stirring, for 1 minute or until fragrant. Remove from heat. Blend or process cumin with remaining ingredients until smooth.

**prep + cook time** 8 hours 30 minutes
**serves** 6 (3.5-litre cooker) or 2–3 (1.5-litre cooker)
**freezing** Korma paste is suitable to freeze.

# Lamb & rosemary stew

**for a 3.5-litre cooker:**
1.2kg lamb neck chops
50g plain flour
2 tablespoons olive oil
250ml dry red wine
3 small brown onions (240g), sliced thickly
3 medium potatoes (600g), sliced thickly
2 medium carrots (240g), sliced thickly
2 tablespoons tomato paste
2 tablespoons finely chopped rosemary
250ml beef stock

**for a 1.5-litre cooker:**
400g lamb neck chops
20g plain flour
3 teaspoons olive oil
85ml dry red wine
1 small brown onion (80g), sliced thickly
1 medium potato (200g), sliced thickly
1 medium carrot (80g), sliced thickly
3 teaspoons tomato paste
1 tablespoon finely chopped rosemary
85ml beef stock

**method:**

**1** Toss lamb in flour to coat; shake off excess. Heat half the oil in a large frying pan over medium-high heat; cook lamb, in batches, until browned. Transfer to a slow cooker.

**2** Add wine to the same pan; bring to the boil. Boil, stirring occasionally, for about 5 minutes or until liquid is reduced by half. Transfer to slow cooker. Add onion, potato, carrot, paste, rosemary and stock. Cook, covered, on low, for 8 hours.

**3** Divide lamb and vegetables among plates. Spoon over a little cooking liquid to serve.

**prep + cook time** 8 hours 45 minutes
**serves** 4 (3.5-litre cooker) or 2 (1.5-litre cooker)
**freezing** Suitable to freeze at the end of step 2.

# Cassoulet

**for a 3.5-litre cooker:**
100g piece smoked streaky bacon
2 tablespoons olive oil
3 thick pork sausages (360g)
900g boned lamb shoulder
1 large brown onion (200g), chopped finely
1 bay leaf
5 cloves garlic, chopped finely
800g canned chopped tomatoes
250ml water
2 tablespoons tomato paste
800g canned white beans, rinsed, drained
2 tablespoons finely chopped fresh flat-leaf parsley

**for a 1.5-litre cooker:**
35g piece smoked streaky bacon
3 teaspoons olive oil
1 thick pork sausage (120g)
300g boned lamb shoulder
1 medium brown onion (65g), chopped finely
1 bay leaf
2 cloves garlic, chopped finely
270g canned chopped tomatoes
85ml water
3 teaspoons tomato paste
270g canned white beans, rinsed, drained
1 tablespoon finely chopped fresh flat-leaf parsley

**method:**
**1** Discard the rind from the pork. Cut the pork into 3cm squares.
**2** Heat half the oil in a large frying pan over medium-high heat; cook sausages and pork, turning, until browned. Transfer to a slow cooker.
**3** Cut the lamb into 3cm pieces. Heat the same pan over medium-high heat; cook lamb, in batches, until browned. Transfer to slow cooker. Drain fat from pan.
**4** Heat remaining oil in the same pan over medium heat; cook onion and bay leaf, stirring, for 5 minutes or until onion softens. Add garlic; cook, stirring, for 1 minute or until fragrant. Transfer to slow cooker.
**5** Add tomatoes, the water, paste and beans to cooker. Cook, covered, on low, for 8 hours. Serve sprinkled with parsley.

**prep + cook time** 8 hours 45 minutes
**serves** 6 (3.5-litre cooker) or 2–3 (1.5-litre cooker)
**freezing** Suitable to freeze at the end of step 5.
**tips** Ask your butcher for a piece of smoked bacon or use the equivalent weight of lardons, instead. You can also lightly toast some breadcrumbs and combine these with the parsley to sprinkle over the cassoulet.

# Sun-dried tomato & balsamic lamb stew

**for a 3.5-litre cooker:**
8 lamb neck chops (1.4kg)
400g canned chopped tomatoes
1 medium red onion (170g), sliced thinly
2 cloves garlic, crushed
250ml beef stock
125ml dry red wine
80ml balsamic vinegar
75g coarsely chopped sun-dried tomatoes
3 tablespoons fresh basil leaves
2 sprigs fresh thyme
340g jar marinated artichoke hearts, drained
2 teaspoons cornflour
1 tablespoon water
3 tablespoons fresh basil leaves, extra

**for a 1.5-litre cooker:**
2 lamb neck chops (460g)
135g canned chopped tomatoes
1 small red onion (55g), sliced thinly
1 clove garlic, crushed
85ml beef stock
45ml dry red wine
30ml balsamic vinegar
25g coarsely chopped sun-dried tomatoes
1 tablespoon fresh basil leaves
1 sprig fresh thyme
115g marinated artichoke hearts, drained
1 teaspoon cornflour
2 teaspoons water
1 tablespoon fresh basil leaves, extra

**method:**

**1** Combine lamb, tomatoes, onion, garlic, stock, wine, vinegar, sun-dried tomatoes and herbs in a slow cooker. Cook, covered, on low, for 8 hours.

**2** Discard thyme from cooker; stir in artichokes. Combine cornflour with the water in a small cup; stir into cooker. Cook, covered, on high, for 10 minutes or until thickened slightly. Season to taste.

**3** Serve stew sprinkled with extra basil.

**prep + cook time** 8 hours 45 minutes
**serves** 4 (3.5-litre cooker) or 2 (1.5-litre cooker)
**freezing** Suitable to freeze.
**tip** We used red wine but you can use white wine if you prefer.

# Lancashire hot pot

**for a 3.5-litre cooker:**
800g boned lamb shoulder
50g plain flour
2 tablespoons olive oil
2 medium brown onions (300g), chopped coarsely
2 cloves garlic, chopped coarsely
125ml dry red wine
2 medium carrots (240g), chopped coarsely
200g button mushrooms, halved
1 tablespoon fresh thyme leaves
1 tablespoon worcestershire sauce
500g potatoes

**for a 1.5-litre cooker:**
270g boned lamb shoulder
20g plain flour
3 teaspoons olive oil
1 medium brown onion (100g), chopped coarsely
1 clove garlic, chopped coarsely
45ml dry red wine
1 medium carrot (80g), chopped coarsely
65g button mushrooms, halved
2 teaspoons fresh thyme leaves
2 teaspoons worcestershire sauce
165g potatoes

**method:**

**1** Cut lamb into 3cm pieces. Toss in flour to coat, shake off excess. Heat half the oil in a large frying pan over medium-high heat; cook lamb, in batches, until browned. Transfer to a slow cooker.

**2** Heat remaining oil in the same pan; cook onion and garlic, stirring, for 5 minutes or until onion softens. Transfer to slow cooker.

**3** Heat same pan; add wine, bring to the boil. Transfer to cooker with carrot, mushrooms, thyme and sauce; stir to combine.

**4** Thinly slice potatoes. Arrange potato slices, slightly overlapping, over lamb mixture. Cook, covered, on low, for 8 hours. Season to taste.

**prep + cook time** 8 hours 30 minutes
**serves** 4 (3.5-litre cooker) or 2 (1.5-litre cooker)
**freezing** Not suitable to freeze.
**tip** If you have one, try using a mandoline to cut the potatoes into paper-thin slices, otherwise, use a very sharp knife.

# Honey-soy lamb chops

**for a 3.5-litre cooker:**
60ml reduced-salt soy sauce
90g honey
3 cloves garlic, crushed
1 teaspoon sesame oil
2 large red onions (600g), cut into thick wedges
6 lamb chops (1.2kg)
6 sprigs fresh rosemary
15g butter, melted
1 tablespoon plain flour

**for a 1.5-litre cooker:**
20ml reduced-salt soy sauce
30g honey
1 clove garlic, crushed
½ teaspoon sesame oil
1 medium red onion (200g), cut into thick wedges
2–3 lamb chops (400g)
2 sprigs fresh rosemary
knob butter, melted
2 teaspoons plain flour

**method:**

**1** Combine sauce, honey, garlic and oil in small jug.

**2** Place onion in a slow cooker; top with lamb, soy sauce mixture and rosemary. Cook, covered, on low, 6 hours.

**3** Discard rosemary, remove lamb from cooker; cover to keep warm.

**4** Combine butter and flour in small bowl; stir into cooker. Cook, covered, on high, about 25 minutes or until sauce thickens; season to taste. Strain sauce through fine sieve into medium heatproof jug; discard onion.

**5** Serve lamb drizzled with sauce.

**prep + cook time** 6 hours 45 minutes
**serves** 6 (3.5-litre cooker) or 2–3 (1.5-litre cooker)
**freezing** Suitable to freeze at the end of step 2.

# Shepherd's pie

**for a 3.5-litre cooker:**
3 medium carrots (360g), chopped coarsely
3 stalks celery (450g), trimmed, chopped coarsely
1 large brown onion (200g), chopped coarsely
2 cloves garlic, crushed
4 sprigs fresh thyme
2 sprigs fresh rosemary
70g tomato paste
2 tablespoons worcestershire sauce
625ml beef stock
1.5kg lamb shoulder
60g frozen peas
150g baby spinach leaves
1 tablespoon cornflour
1 tablespoon water
800g potatoes, chopped coarsely
40g butter
125ml hot milk
60g coarsely grated cheddar

**for a 1.5-litre cooker:**
1 medium carrot (120g), chopped coarsely
1 stalk celery (150g), trimmed, chopped coarsely
1 medium brown onion (65g), chopped coarsely
1 clove garlic, crushed
2 sprigs fresh thyme
1 sprig fresh rosemary
25g tomato paste
3 teaspoons worcestershire sauce
210ml beef stock
500g lamb shoulder
20g frozen peas
50g baby spinach leaves
2 teaspoons cornflour
2 teaspoons water
270g potatoes, chopped coarsely
15g butter
45ml hot milk
20g coarsely grated cheddar

**method:**

**1** Combine carrot, celery, onion, garlic, herbs, paste, sauce and stock in a slow cooker. Add lamb, turn to coat in mixture. Cook, covered, on high for 2 hours. Reduce to low; cook for 8 hours.

**2** Remove lamb from cooker; shred meat coarsely, discard fat and bones. Discard herbs from cooker. Return lamb to cooker with peas and spinach. Blend cornflour and the water in a small cup, stir into the cooker; cook, uncovered, on high, for 20 minutes or until thickened. Season to taste.

**3** Meanwhile, boil, steam or microwave potato until tender; drain. Mash potato with butter and hot milk until smooth; season to taste.

**4** Preheat grill.

**5** Transfer lamb to a 2.5-litre ovenproof dish (if using a 3.5-litre cooker) or a 1-litre ovenproof dish (if using a 1.5-litre cooker). Spoon potato over lamb mixture; sprinkle with cheese. Grill for 5 minutes or until top is browned lightly.

**prep + cook time** 11 hours
**serves** 4 (3.5-litre cooker) or 2 (1.5-litre cooker)
**freezing** Suitable to freeze.

# Panang lamb curry

**for a 3.5-litre cooker:**
1.5kg boneless lamb shoulder
1 tablespoon groundnut oil
150g panang curry paste
625ml coconut cream
2 tablespoons fish sauce
65g grated palm sugar
2 tablespoons peanut butter
4 fresh kaffir lime leaves
225g canned sliced bamboo shoots, drained, rinsed
1 small red pepper (150g), sliced thinly
200g green beans, trimmed, halved
6 tablespoons fresh coriander leaves

**for a 1.5-litre cooker:**
500g boneless lamb shoulder
2 teaspoons groundnut oil
50g panang curry paste
210ml coconut cream
3 teaspoons fish sauce
25g grated palm sugar
3 teaspoons peanut butter
2 fresh kaffir lime leaves
75g canned sliced bamboo shoots, drained, rinsed
½ small red pepper (50g), sliced thinly
65g green beans, trimmed, halved
3 tablespoons fresh coriander leaves

**method:**

**1** Cut lamb into 5cm pieces. Heat oil in a large frying pan; cook lamb, in batches, until browned. Transfer to a slow cooker.

**2** Cook paste in same pan, stirring, 1 minute or until fragrant. Add coconut cream, sauce, sugar, peanut butter and lime leaves; bring to the boil. Transfer to cooker.

**3** Cook, covered, on low, 3½ hours. Add bamboo shoots, pepper and beans to cooker; cook, covered, on low, 30 minutes or until vegetables are tender. Season to taste.

**4** Serve curry topped with coriander.

**prep + cook time** 4 hours 30 minutes
**serves** 8 (3.5-litre cooker) or 3–4 (1.5-litre cooker)
**freezing** Not suitable to freeze.
**tip** If you can't find panang curry paste, you can use thai red curry or massaman curry paste instead.

# Lamb tagine with harissa & green olives

**for a 3.5-litre cooker:**
1.2kg boned lamb shoulder, chopped coarsely
1 large red onion (300g), grated coarsely
2 cloves garlic, crushed
2 tablespoons finely chopped coriander stems
1 cinnamon stick, halved
1 teaspoon ground cumin
1 teaspoon ground ginger
1 teaspoon sweet paprika
80ml olive oil
1 tablespoon harissa paste
800g canned chopped tomatoes
70g tomato paste
125ml beef stock
400g canned chickpeas, rinsed, drained
2 tablespoons honey
90g pitted small green olives
2 teaspoons finely chopped preserved lemon rind
6 tablespoons fresh mint leaves

**for a 1.5-litre cooker:**
400g boned lamb shoulder, chopped coarsely
1 medium red onion (100g), grated coarsely
1 clove garlic, crushed
1 tablespoon finely chopped coriander stems
½ cinnamon stick
½ teaspoon ground cumin
½ teaspoon ground ginger
½ teaspoon sweet paprika
30ml olive oil
2 teaspoons harissa paste
270g canned chopped tomatoes
25g tomato paste
45ml beef stock
135g canned chickpeas, rinsed, drained
3 teaspoons honey
30g pitted small green olives
1 teaspoon finely chopped preserved lemon rind
3 tablespoons fresh mint leaves

**method:**
**1** Combine lamb, onion, garlic, coriander stems, spices and half the oil in large bowl.
**2** Heat remaining oil in large frying pan; cook lamb mixture, in batches, until browned all over. Transfer lamb to a slow cooker.
**3** Stir harissa paste, tomatoes, tomato paste, stock, chickpeas and honey into cooker. Cook, covered, on low, 4 hours.
**4** Remove cinnamon stick; stir in olives and lemon rind. Season to taste; sprinkle with mint.

**prep + cook time** 4 hours 30 minutes
**serves** 6 (3.5-litre cooker) or 2–3 (1.5-litre cooker)
**freezing** Suitable to freeze at the end of step 3.
**tip** Preserved lemon rind is available at most supermarkets. Remove and discard the flesh, wash the rind, then use it as the recipe directs.

# Vegetables

# Quinoa-stuffed peppers

**for a 3.5-litre cooker:**
2 tablespoons olive oil
1 medium brown onion (150g), chopped finely
3 cloves garlic, crushed
2 tablespoons tomato paste
280g passata
150g quinoa
250ml chicken stock
400g canned brown lentils, rinsed, drained
180g feta cheese, crumbled
50g pitted black olives, finely chopped
3 tablespoons coarsely chopped fresh flat-leaf parsley
3 tablespoons coarsely chopped fresh basil
5 medium peppers (1kg)

for a 1.5-litre cooker:
3 teaspoons olive oil
1 small brown onion (50g), chopped finely
1 clove garlic, crushed
3 teaspoons tomato paste
95g passata
50g quinoa
85ml chicken stock
135g canned brown lentils, rinsed, drained
60g feta cheese, crumbled
20g pitted black olives, finely chopped
1 tablespoon coarsely chopped fresh flat-leaf parsley
1 tablespoon coarsely chopped fresh basil
2 medium peppers (330g)

**method:**

**1** Heat oil in a large frying pan over medium heat; cook onion and garlic, stirring, for 5 minutes or until onion softens. Add paste, passata, quinoa and stock; bring to the boil. Remove from heat. Stir in lentils, cheese, olives and herbs. Season to taste.

**2** Cut tops from each pepper; reserve tops. Using a small spoon, scoop out the membranes and seeds. Trim a little off bases to level if necessary so that the peppers stand upright in the slow cooker. Divide quinoa mixture among the peppers; replace the tops.

**3** Place the peppers into a slow cooker. Cook, covered, on high, for 3 hours.

**prep + cook time** 3 hours 45 minutes
**makes** 5 (3.5-litre cooker) or 2 (1.5-litre cooker)
**freezing** Not suitable to freeze.
**tip** Choose peppers that are taller rather than wider, so they all fit into the slow cooker.

# Spinach & three cheese cannelloni

**for a 3.5-litre cooker:**
750g frozen spinach, thawed
840g ricotta cheese
2 eggs
1 egg yolk
60g finely grated parmesan cheese
225g bottled char-grilled aubergine in olive oil, drained, chopped finely
3 cloves garlic, crushed
1 litre passata
180ml single cream
handful coarsely chopped fresh basil
400g dried cannelloni tubes
180g grated mozzarella

**for a 1.5-litre cooker:**
250g frozen spinach, thawed
280g ricotta cheese
1 egg
20g finely grated parmesan cheese
75g bottled char-grilled aubergine in olive oil, drained, chopped finely
1 clove garlic, crushed
330ml passata
60ml single cream
2 tablespoons coarsely chopped fresh basil
135g dried cannelloni tubes
60g grated mozzarella

**method:**

**1** Squeeze excess moisture from the spinach. Place spinach, ricotta, eggs, egg yolk (if using a 3.5-litre cooker), parmesan, aubergine and garlic in a large bowl; stir to combine. Season.

**2** Combine passata, cream and basil in a large jug; season.

**3** Lightly oil a slow cooker. Pour half the passata mixture over base of the cooker.

**4** Spoon or pipe spinach mixture into cannelloni tubes; arrange cannelloni vertically in cooker. Top with remaining passata mixture; sprinkle with mozzarella. Cook, covered, on low, for 4 hours. Stand for 10 minutes before serving.

**prep + cook time** 5 hours
**serves** 6 (3.5-litre cooker) or 2–3 (1.5-litre cooker)
**freezing** Not suitable to freeze.

# Cauliflower cheese

**for a 3.5-litre cooker:**
- 50g butter, chopped coarsely
- 2 tablespoons plain flour
- 500ml milk
- 150g grated Gruyère
- 1 medium cauliflower (1.5kg), cut into florets
- 1 medium brown onion (150g), chopped finely
- 40g finely grated parmesan cheese
- 25g flaked almonds
- 3 tablespoons coarsely chopped fresh flat-leaf parsley

**for a 1.5-litre cooker:**
- 20g butter, chopped coarsely
- 3 teaspoons plain flour
- 165ml milk
- 50g grated Gruyère
- 1 small cauliflower (500g), cut into florets
- 1 small brown onion (50g), chopped finely
- 15g finely grated parmesan cheese
- 10g flaked almonds
- 1 tablespoon coarsely chopped fresh flat-leaf parsley

**method:**

**1** Melt butter in a medium saucepan over medium heat, add flour; cook, stirring, for about 2 minutes or until mixture thickens and bubbles. Gradually stir in milk; cook, stirring, until sauce boils and thickens. Remove from heat; stir in Gruyère until melted.

**2** Place cauliflower and onion into a slow cooker; toss to combine. Season to taste. Pour over cheese sauce; toss to coat. Sprinkle with parmesan.

**3** Cook, covered, on low, for 3 hours. Sprinkle with nuts and parsley to serve.

**prep + cook time** 3 hours 30 minutes
**serves** 6 (3.5-litre cooker) or 2–3 (1.5-litre cooker)
**freezing** Not suitable to freeze.

# Pumpkin, sage & courgette lasagne

**for a 3.5-litre cooker:**
1kg pumpkin, chopped coarsely
60g butter, chopped
5 cloves garlic, crushed
1½ tablespoons finely chopped fresh sage
720g ricotta cheese
1 egg
¼ teaspoon ground nutmeg
80g finely grated parmesan cheese
3 medium courgettes (360g)
cooking-oil spray
80ml single cream
8 dried lasagne sheets (120g)
100g coarsely grated mozzarella cheese

**for a 1.5-litre cooker:**
330g pumpkin, chopped coarsely
20g butter, chopped
2 cloves garlic, crushed
2 teaspoons finely chopped fresh sage
240g ricotta cheese
1 small egg
pinch ground nutmeg
30g finely grated parmesan cheese
1 medium courgette (120g)
cooking-oil spray
60ml single cream
3 dried lasagne sheets (60g)
35g coarsely grated mozzarella cheese

**prep + cook time** 4 hours 45 minutes
**serves** 6 (3.5-litre cooker) or 2 (1.5-litre cooker)
**freezing** Suitable to freeze at the end of step 6.

**method:**

**1** Boil, steam or microwave pumpkin until tender; drain.

**2** Melt butter in a large frying pan over medium heat; cook garlic and sage for 1 minute or until fragrant. Stir in pumpkin; remove from heat. Season.

**3** Combine ricotta, egg, nutmeg and half the parmesan in a large bowl; season.

**4** Thinly slice courgettes lengthways using a vegetable peeler.

**5** Lightly spray a slow cooker with oil. Drizzle 2 tablespoons of cream over base; top with two lasagne sheets for the 3.5-litre cooker or one lasagne sheet for the 1.5-litre cooker, breaking to fit.

**6** Spread one-third of the pumpkin mixture over pasta; top with one-third of the courgette slices, then one-quarter of the ricotta mixture. Top with two (or one, if using 1.5-litre cooker) more lasagne sheets. Repeat layering, finishing with pasta. Pour over the remaining cream, then spread with the remaining ricotta mixture. Sprinkle with mozzarella and remaining parmesan. Cook, covered, on low, for 4 hours or until pasta is tender.

# Aubergine, chilli & tomato stew with feta

**for a 3.5-litre cooker:**
2 celery stalks (300g), trimmed
4 cloves garlic, sliced thinly
1 fresh red chilli, sliced thinly
800g canned cherry tomatoes
2 medium red onions (340g), unpeeled
60ml olive oil
2 medium aubergines (600g)
400g piece feta cheese
½ teaspoon dried chilli flakes
2 teaspoons olive oil, extra
3 tablespoons fresh basil leaves

**for a 1.5-litre cooker:**
1 celery stalk (100g), trimmed
2 cloves garlic, sliced thinly
½ fresh red chilli, sliced thinly
270g canned cherry tomatoes
1 medium red onion (115g), unpeeled
20ml olive oil
1 medium aubergine (200g)
135g piece feta cheese
pinch dried chilli flakes
1 teaspoon olive oil, extra
1 tablespoon fresh basil leaves

**prep + cook time** 2 hours 45 minutes
**serves** 4 (3.5-litre cooker) or 2 (1.5-litre cooker)
**freezing** Not suitable to freeze.
**tip** Canned cherry tomatoes are available from most supermarkets. You can use canned chopped tomatoes instead.

**method:**
**1** Cut celery into 7.5cm lengths. Place garlic, chilli, celery and tomatoes in a slow cooker. Season.
**2** Peel onions leaving root end intact. Cut each onion into eight wedges.
**3** Heat half the oil in a medium frying pan over medium-high heat; cook onion, turning, until browned. Transfer to cooker.
**4** Meanwhile, chop aubergines into 5cm pieces. Heat remaining oil in the same pan over medium heat; cook aubergines, turning occasionally, until browned. Transfer to cooker.
**5** Cook, covered, on high, for 2 hours. Season to taste.
**6** Cut feta into chunks; place on serving platter. Sprinkle with chilli; drizzle with extra oil.
**7** To serve, sprinkle aubergine stew with basil; accompany with feta chunks.

# Ratatouille

**for a 3.5-litre cooker:**
2 tablespoons olive oil
1 large red onion (300g), chopped coarsely
3 cloves garlic, crushed
6 tablespoons fresh basil leaves
2 tablespoons tomato paste
700g passata
2 teaspoons caster sugar
1 large aubergine (500g), chopped coarsely
2 medium red peppers (400g), chopped coarsely
2 large courgettes (300g), chopped coarsely
1 medium green pepper (200g), chopped coarsely

**for a 1.5-litre cooker:**
3 teaspoons olive oil
1 medium red onion (100g), chopped coarsely
1 clove garlic, crushed
2 tablespoons fresh basil leaves
3 teaspoons tomato paste
230g passata
1 teaspoon caster sugar
1 medium aubergine (165g), chopped coarsely
1 small red pepper (135g), chopped coarsely
1 medium courgette (100g), chopped coarsely
½ small green pepper (65g), chopped coarsely

**method:**
**1** Heat oil in large frying pan; cook onion, garlic and half the basil, stirring, until onion softens. Add paste; cook, stirring, 1 minute. Remove from heat, stir in passata and sugar.
**2** Place vegetables and sauce mixture into a slow cooker. Cook, covered, on low, 4 hours. Season to taste.
**3** Serve ratatouille sprinkled with remaining basil.

**prep + cook time** 4 hours 30 minutes
**serves** 6 (3.5-litre cooker) or 2–3 (1.5-litre cooker)
**freezing** Suitable to freeze at the end of step 2, although it's much better eaten straight after cooking.

# Artichokes with garlic anchovy crumbs

**for a 3.5-litre cooker:**
6 medium globe artichokes (1.2kg)
2 litres water
500ml chicken stock
2 tablespoons lemon juice
60ml olive oil

**garlic anchovy crumbs**
1 tablespoon olive oil
6 anchovy fillets, drained, chopped finely
3 cloves garlic, crushed
105g stale breadcrumbs
1 tablespoon finely grated lemon rind
4 tablespoons finely chopped fresh flat-leaf parsley
40g finely grated pecorino romano cheese

**prep + cook time** 8 hours 30 minutes
**serves** 6 (3.5-litre cooker) or 2 (1.5-litre cooker) as a starter
**freezing** Not suitable to freeze.
**tip** Serve with some crusty bread and a green or tomato salad to make a main meal.

**for a 1.5-litre cooker:**
2 medium globe artichokes (400g)
670ml litres water
165ml chicken stock
3 teaspoons lemon juice
20ml olive oil

**garlic anchovy crumbs**
2 teaspoons olive oil
2 anchovy fillets, drained, chopped finely
1 clove garlic, crushed
35g stale breadcrumbs
2 teaspoons finely grated lemon rind
2 tablespoons finely chopped fresh flat-leaf parsley
15g finely grated pecorino romano cheese

**method:**
**1** Remove and discard tough outer leaves from artichokes. Trim stems so that artichoke bases sit flat. Using a small teaspoon, remove and discard hairy chokes from centre of artichokes; rinse artichokes under cold water.
**2** Pack artichokes tightly, upside down, into a slow cooker; pour in the water, stock and juice. Cook, covered, on low, 8 hours.
**3** Make garlic anchovy crumbs before serving.
**4** Remove artichokes with slotted spoon; drain well. Serve artichokes with olive oil and garlic anchovy crumbs for dipping.

**garlic anchovy crumbs** Heat oil in large frying pan; cook anchovy and garlic, stirring, until anchovy softens. Add breadcrumbs and rind; cook, stirring, until crumbs are browned lightly and crisp. Transfer to medium bowl; cool. Stir in parsley and cheese; season to taste.

Pepper mash
Sweet potato mash
Potato & celeriac mash
Fennel mash
Pea mash
Spinach mash

# Vegetable mashes

## Pepper mash

Quarter 2 red peppers; discard seeds and membranes. Roast under hot grill, skin-side up, until skin blisters and blackens. Cover peppers with plastic or paper for 5 minutes, then peel away skin; chop flesh coarsely. Blend peppers until smooth. Meanwhile, boil, steam or microwave 1kg coarsely chopped potatoes until tender, drain. Mash potato in large bowl; stir in 125ml hot single cream and 20g softened butter. Add pepper to mash; stir until combined. Season to taste.

**prep + cook time** 30 minutes
**serves** 4

## Sweet potato mash

Coarsely chop 500g sweet potato and 500g potatoes; boil, steam or microwave together, until tender; drain. Mash in large bowl; stir in 60ml hot chicken stock and 40g melted butter. Season to taste.

**prep + cook time** 30 minutes
**serves** 4

## Potato & celeriac mash

Coarsely chop 800g potatoes and 1kg celeriac; boil, steam or microwave potato and celeriac, separately, until tender; drain. Mash potato and celeriac in large bowl; stir in 125ml hot single cream and 60g softened butter. Season to taste.

**prep + cook time** 30 minutes
**serves** 4

## Fennel mash

Slice 1 large fennel bulb thinly. Melt 60g butter in large frying pan; cook fennel, covered, over low heat, about 10 minutes or until fennel is very soft. Blend or process fennel until smooth. Meanwhile, boil, steam or microwave 1kg coarsely chopped potatoes until tender; drain. Mash potato in large bowl; stir in fennel mixture and 125ml hot single cream. Season to taste.

**prep + cook time** 30 minutes
**serves** 4

## Pea mash

Coarsely chop 1kg potatoes; boil, steam or microwave potato and 200g frozen peas, separately, until tender; drain. Mash potato in large bowl; stir in 185ml hot milk and 50g softened butter. Using fork, mash peas in small bowl; stir into potato mixture. Season to taste.

**prep + cook time** 30 minutes
**serves** 4

## Spinach mash

Coarsely chop 1kg potatoes; boil, steam or microwave until tender, drain. Meanwhile, boil, steam or microwave 220g trimmed spinach leaves until wilted; drain. When cool enough to handle, squeeze out excess liquid. Blend or process spinach with 40g softened butter until almost smooth. Mash potato in large bowl; stir in 125ml hot single cream and spinach mixture. Season to taste.

**prep + cook time** 30 minutes
**serves** 4

# Desserts

# Chocolate & cherry puddings

**for a 3.5-litre cooker:**
125g butter, softened
165g caster sugar
1 teaspoon vanilla extract
2 eggs
110g self-raising flour
50g cocoa powder
60ml milk
60g dark chocolate, chopped finely
670g pitted morello or black cherries in syrup, drained
80ml double cream

for a 1.5-litre cooker:
30g butter, softened
40g caster sugar
¼ teaspoon vanilla extract
1 small egg
30g self-raising flour
15g cocoa powder
15ml milk
15g dark chocolate, chopped finely
170g pitted morello or black cherries in syrup, drained
20ml double cream

**method:**

**1** Grease four 250ml deep heatproof dishes for the 3.5-litre cooker and one for the 1.5-litre cooker.

**2** Beat butter, sugar and extract in a small bowl with an electric mixer until light and fluffy. Beat in eggs, one at a time. Stir in the sifted dry ingredients then the milk and chocolate. Fold in half the cherries. Divide mixture between dishes.

**3** Place dishes in a slow cooker. Pour in enough boiling water to come halfway up the side of the dishes. Cook, covered, on high, for about 1½ hours or until mixture is firm. Remove puddings from cooker; dust with extra cocoa if you like and serve with cream and remaining cherries.

**prep + cook time** 1 hour 45 minutes
**makes** 4 (3.5-litre cooker) or 1 (1.5-litre cooker)
**freezing** Not suitable to freeze.
**tip** Ensure the heatproof dishes fit into your slow cooker before you begin.

# Caramel mud cake

**for a 3.5-litre cooker:**
180g white chocolate, chopped finely
60g unsalted butter, chopped finely
5 eggs, separated
2 teaspoons vanilla extract
60g ground almonds
35g self-raising flour
75g dark brown sugar

**caramel icing**
60g unsalted butter, chopped
110g dark brown sugar
125ml milk
110g icing sugar

**for a 1.5-litre cooker:**
60g white chocolate, chopped finely
20g unsalted butter, chopped finely
2 eggs, separated
½ teaspoon vanilla extract
20g ground almonds
1 heaped tablespoon self-raising flour
25g dark brown sugar

**caramel icing**
20g unsalted butter, chopped
40g dark brown sugar
45ml milk
40g icing sugar

**method:**

**1** Grease a 2-litre pudding basin for a 3.5-litre cooker or a 600ml pudding basin for a 1.5-litre cooker; line base with baking parchment.

**2** Combine chocolate and butter in a medium saucepan; stir over low heat until smooth. Remove from heat; cool for 10 minutes. Stir egg yolks and extract, then ground almonds and sifted flour into chocolate mixture.

**3** Beat egg whites in a small bowl with an electric mixer until soft peaks form; add sugar and beat until sugar dissolves. Fold egg white mixture into chocolate mixture in two batches. Spoon mixture into the pudding basin.

**4** Place basin, without lid, in a slow cooker with enough boiling water to come halfway up side of basin. Cook, covered, on high, for about 2 hours (for a 3.5-litre cooker) or 1½ hours (for a 1.5-litre cooker) or until firm.

**5** Remove cake from the cooker. Immediately turn onto a baking-parchment-lined wire rack; cool completely.

**6** Make caramel icing. Spread cake with icing.

**caramel icing** Melt butter in a small saucepan over medium heat. Add brown sugar and milk; cook, stirring, over medium heat until sugar dissolves. Bring to the boil. Reduce heat; simmer for 1 minute. Remove from heat. Whisk in sifted icing sugar until smooth.

**prep + cook time** 2 hours 30 minutes (for a 3.5-litre cooker) or 2 hours (for a 1.5-litre cooker) + cooling time
**serves** 12 (3.5-litre cooker) or 4 (1.5-litre cooker)
**freezing** Suitable to freeze at the end of step 6.
**tip** Ensure that the pudding basin fits into your slow cooker before you begin.

# Spanish caramel rice pudding

**for a 3.5-litre cooker:**
15g butter
175g arborio rice
1 litre milk
250ml water
1 cinnamon stick
1 vanilla pod, split, seeds scraped
1 x 397g can caramel filling
40g sultanas
125ml sweet sherry
½ teaspoon finely grated orange rind
50g flaked almonds, toasted

**for a 1.5-litre cooker:**
10g butter
90g arborio rice
500ml milk
125ml water
½ cinnamon stick
½ vanilla pod, split, seeds scraped
½ x 397g can caramel filling
20g sultanas
65ml sweet sherry
½ teaspoon finely grated orange rind
25g flaked almonds, toasted

**method:**

**1** Melt butter in a large saucepan over medium heat. Add rice; stir 2 minutes to coat well. Stir in milk, the water, cinnamon, vanilla pod and seeds; bring mixture to the boil.

**2** Meanwhile, spoon caramel into a slow cooker; whisk until smooth. Add rice mixture to caramel; whisk well to combine. Cover surface of pudding with baking parchment. Cook, covered, on high, for about 2¼ hours, stirring twice during cooking, or until rice is tender and liquid thickened.

**3** Meanwhile, combine sultanas and sherry in a small saucepan; bring to a boil. Reduce heat to medium; cook mixture for about 5 minutes or until liquid is reduced by half. Stir in orange rind and set aside until needed.

**4** Discard cinnamon stick and vanilla pod. Serve rice pudding warm or chilled, topped with sherry sultana mixture and almonds.

**prep + cook time** 2 hours 45 minutes
**serves** 4 (3.5-litre cooker) or 2 (1.5-litre cooker)
**freezing** Not suitable to freeze.
**tip** Leftover rice pudding will keep refrigerated for up to 1 week.

# Mandarin & almond pudding

**for a 3.5-litre cooker:**
4 small mandarin oranges (400g)
4 eggs
150g caster sugar
160g ground almonds
100g self-raising flour

**for a 1.5-litre cooker:**
1 small mandarin orange (100g)
1 egg
40g caster sugar
40g ground almonds
25g self-raising flour

**method:**

**1** Place washed unpeeled mandarins in a slow cooker; cover with hot water. Cook, covered, on high, 2 hours.

**2** Trim ends from mandarins; discard. Halve mandarins; remove and discard seeds. Process mandarins, including rind, until mixture is pulpy.

**3** Grease 2-litre pudding basin for a 3.5-litre cooker or 500-ml basin for a 1.5-litre cooker.

**4** Beat eggs and sugar in small bowl with electric mixer until thick and creamy; fold in ground almonds, sifted flour and mandarin pulp. Spoon mixture into steamer. Top with pleated baking parchment and foil; secure with kitchen string or lid.

**5** Place pudding in cooker with enough boiling water to come halfway up side of basin. Cook, covered, on high, 3 hours (for a 3.5-litre cooker) or 2 hours (for a 1.5-litre cooker), replenishing with boiling water as necessary to maintain level. Stand pudding 5 minutes before turning onto plate.

**prep + cook time** 5 hours 30 minutes (for a 3.5-litre cooker) or 4 hours 30 minutes (for a 1.5-litre cooker)
**serves** 8 (3.5-litre cooker) or 2 (1.5-litre cooker)
**freezing** Not suitable to freeze.
**tip** The pleated baking parchment and foil simply allow space for the pudding mixture to rise. Ensure that the pudding basin fits into your slow cooker before you begin.

# Delicious lemony lime puddings

**for a 3.5-litre cooker:**
90g butter, melted
1 teaspoon finely grated lemon rind
½ teaspoon finely grated lime rind
165g caster sugar
2 eggs, separated
50g self-raising flour
2 tablespoons lemon juice
1 tablespoon lime juice
250ml milk

**for a 1.5-litre cooker:**
25g butter, melted
½ teaspoon finely grated lemon rind
¼ teaspoon finely grated lime rind
40g caster sugar
1 small egg, separated
15g self-raising flour
2 teaspoons lemon juice
1 teaspoon lime juice
65ml milk

**method:**
**1** Grease four 180ml deep heatproof dishes for a 3.5-litre cooker or one for a 1.5-litre cooker.
**2** Combine butter, rinds, sugar and egg yolks in medium bowl. Whisk in sifted flour, then juices. Gradually whisk in milk; mixture should be smooth and runny.
**3** Beat egg whites in small bowl with electric mixer until soft peaks form; fold into lemon mixture, in two batches. Divide mixture between dishes.
**4** Place dishes in a slow cooker; pour enough boiling water into cooker to come halfway up sides of dishes. Cook, covered, on high, about 1 hour or until firm. Remove dishes from cooker. Stand puddings 10 minutes before serving.

**prep + cook time** 1 hour 30 minutes
**makes** 4 (3.5-litre cooker) or 1 (1.5-litre cooker)
**freezing** Not suitable to freeze.
**tip** Make sure that the heatproof dishes fit into your slow cooker before you begin.

# Mixed berry pudding

**for a 3.5-litre cooker:**
90g butter
180ml milk
1 teaspoon vanilla extract
110g caster sugar
250g self-raising flour
1 egg, beaten lightly
500g frozen mixed berries
160g raspberry jam
500ml boiling water

**for a 1.5-litre cooker:**
45g butter
90ml milk
½ teaspoon vanilla extract
55g caster sugar
125g self-raising flour
1 small egg, beaten lightly
250g frozen mixed berries
80g raspberry jam
250ml boiling water

**method:**
**1** Grease a slow cooker bowl.
**2** Heat butter and milk in medium saucepan over low heat until butter is melted. Remove from heat; cool 5 minutes. Stir in extract and sugar, then sifted flour and egg.
**3** Sprinkle berries over base of cooker bowl; drop tablespoons of jam over berries. Spread pudding mixture over berry mixture. Gently pour the boiling water evenly over pudding mixture. Cook, covered, on high, about 2½ hours (for a 3.5-litre cooker) or 1½ hours (for a 1.5-litre cooker) or until centre of pudding feels firm.
**4** Remove bowl from cooker. Stand pudding 10 minutes before serving.

**prep + cook time** 3 hours (for a 3.5-litre cooker) or 2 hours (for a 1.5-litre cooker)
**serves** 6 (3.5-litre cooker) or 2–3 (1.5-litre cooker)
**freezing** Not suitable to freeze.

# Glossary

**balsamic vinegar** authentic only from the province of Modena, Italy; made from a regional wine of white trebbiano grapes specially processed then aged in antique wooden casks to give the exquisite pungent flavour.

**caraway seeds** a member of the parsley family; available in seed or ground form.

**cayenne pepper** thin-fleshed, long, very-hot red chilli; usually purchased dried and ground.

**celeriac** tuberous root with brown skin, white flesh and a celery-like flavour.

**chickpeas** also called garbanzos, hummus or channa; an irregularly round, sandy-coloured legume.

**chillies** available in many types and sizes, both fresh and dried. The smaller the chilli, the hotter it is. Wear rubber gloves when handling chillies, as they can burn your skin. Removing seeds and membranes lessens the heat level.
**flakes** deep-red in colour; dehydrated, extremely fine slices and whole seeds; good for cooking or for sprinkling over cooked food.
**powder** the Asian variety is the hottest, made from ground chillies; it can be used as a substitute for fresh chillies in the proportion of ½ teaspoon ground chilli powder to 1 medium chopped fresh chilli.

**chorizo** a sausage of Spanish origin; made of coarsely ground pork and seasoned with garlic and chillies.

**cinnamon** dried inner bark of the shoots of the cinnamon tree. Available as a stick or ground.

**coconut**
**milk** unsweetened coconut milk is available in cans.
**water** clear liquid from young green coconuts. It is available natural and flavoured from supermarkets.

**coriander** also known as cilantro or chinese parsley; bright-green-leafed herb with a pungent flavour. The seeds are also available dried and ground. Ground coriander cannot be substituted for fresh, or vice versa.

**cornflour** also known as cornstarch; used as a thickening agent in cooking.

**cumin** available both ground and as whole seeds; cumin has a warm, earthy, rather strong flavour.

**curry leaves** available fresh or dried, they have a mild curry flavour; use like bay leaves.

**curry powder** a blend of ground spices; choose mild or hot to suit your taste and the recipe.

**fennel** bulb vegetable, also known as finocchio or anise. Also the name given to dried seeds having a liquorice flavour.

**fish sauce** also known as nam pla or nuoc nam; made from pulverised salted fermented fish, mostly anchovies. Has a pungent smell and strong taste; use sparingly.

**five-spice powder** a fragrant mixture of ground cinnamon, cloves, star anise, sichuan pepper and fennel seeds.

**garam masala** a blend of spices based on varying proportions of cardamom, cinnamon, cloves, coriander, fennel and cumin, roasted and ground together. Black pepper and chilli can be added for a hotter version.

**ginger**
**fresh** also called green or root ginger; the thick gnarled root of a tropical plant. Can be kept, peeled, covered with dry sherry in a jar and refrigerated, or frozen in an airtight container.

**globe artichokes** a member of the thistle family, they have tough outer leaves, the bases of which can be eaten, an inedible inner 'choke' and a tender heart. The hearts can be purchased in brine canned or in jars.

**harissa paste** a North African spicy paste made from dried red chillies, garlic, olive oil and caraway seeds. It can be used as a rub for meat, an ingredient in sauces and dressings, or eaten on its own as a condiment. It is available, ready-made, from Middle-Eastern food shops and most supermarkets.

**kaffir lime leaves** aromatic leaves used fresh or dried in Asian dishes. A strip of fresh lime peel may be substituted for each kaffir lime leaf.

**moroccan seasoning** a blend of herbs and spices most commonly including cumin, cinnamon and mint. Available in supermarkets, delicatessens and online.

**mushrooms**
**button** small, cultivated white mushrooms with a delicate, subtle flavour.
**chestnut** light to dark brown mushrooms with mild, earthy flavour.
**porcini** firm, nutty-flavoured Italian mushroom. Dried porcini mushrooms are widely available and add a strong flavour to pasta, soups and sauces.

**mustard powder** finely ground white (yellow) mustard seeds.

**nutmeg** dried nut of an evergreen tree; available in ground form or you can grate your own with a fine grater.

**passata** thick sauce made from ripe tomatoes that have been puréed and sieved to remove the skin and seeds.

**paprika** ground dried red pepper; available in sweet, smoked or hot varieties. Sweet paprika is available at delis, speciality food stores and online.

**pine nuts** also known as pignoli; small, cream-coloured kernels obtained from the cones of different varieties of pine trees.

**preserved lemon** a North African specialty, lemons are preserved, usually whole, in a mixture of salt and lemon juice or oil. To use, remove and discard pulp, squeeze juice from rind, then rinse rind well before slicing thinly. Available from specialty food shops, delicatessens and good supermarkets.

**prunes** commercially or sun-dried plums.

**quinoa** pronounced 'keen-wa', these are tiny grains with a firm texture. Quinoa is a complete protein and can be used as an alternative to rice and couscous.

**rice**
**arborio** small, round-grain rice; especially suitable for risottos.
**basmati** fragrant, long-grained white rice. Wash several times before cooking.

**saffron** one of the most expensive spices in the world, true saffron comes only from the saffron crocus, that can produce several flowers a year.

**shallots** small, elongated, brown skinned members of the onion family. Grows in tight clusters similar to garlic.

**star anise** a dried star-shaped pod, the seeds of which taste of aniseed.

**tabasco sauce** brand name of an extremely fiery sauce made from vinegar, hot red peppers and salt. Use sparingly.

**thai basil** sweet, aromatic basil native to Southeast Asia. You can substitute the more common variety, but the taste will not be the same.

# Index

# Conversion charts

## measures

One metric tablespoon holds 20ml; one metric teaspoon holds 5ml.

All cup and spoon measurements are level. The most accurate way of measuring dry ingredients is to weigh them. When measuring liquids, use a clear glass or plastic jug with metric markings.

We use large eggs with an average weight of 60g.

## dry measures

| METRIC | IMPERIAL |
|---|---|
| 15g | ½oz |
| 30g | 1oz |
| 60g | 2oz |
| 90g | 3oz |
| 125g | 4oz (¼lb) |
| 155g | 5oz |
| 185g | 6oz |
| 220g | 7oz |
| 250g | 8oz (½lb) |
| 280g | 9oz |
| 315g | 10oz |
| 345g | 11oz |
| 375g | 12oz (¾lb) |
| 410g | 13oz |
| 440g | 14oz |
| 470g | 15oz |
| 500g | 16oz (1lb) |
| 750g | 24oz (1½lb) |
| 1kg | 32oz (2lb) |

## liquid measures

| METRIC | IMPERIAL |
|---|---|
| 30ml | 1 fluid oz |
| 60ml | 2 fluid oz |
| 100ml | 3 fluid oz |
| 125ml | 4 fluid oz |
| 150ml | 5 fluid oz |
| 190ml | 6 fluid oz |
| 250ml | 8 fluid oz |
| 300ml | 10 fluid oz |
| 500ml | 16 fluid oz |
| 600ml | 20 fluid oz |
| 1000ml (1 litre) | 32 fluid oz |

## length measures

| | |
|---|---|
| 3mm | ⅛in |
| 6mm | ¼in |
| 1cm | ½in |
| 2cm | ¾in |
| 2.5cm | 1in |
| 5cm | 2in |
| 6cm | 2½in |
| 8cm | 3in |
| 10cm | 4in |
| 13cm | 5in |
| 15cm | 6in |
| 18cm | 7in |
| 20cm | 8in |
| 23cm | 9in |
| 25cm | 10in |
| 28cm | 11in |
| 30cm | 12in (1ft) |

## oven temperatures

These are fan-assisted temperatures. If you have a conventional oven (ie. not fan-assisted), increase temperatures by 10–20°.

| | °C (CELSIUS) | °F (FAHRENHEIT) | GAS MARK |
|---|---|---|---|
| Very low | 100 | 210 | ½ |
| Low | 130 | 260 | 1–2 |
| Moderately low | 140 | 280 | 3 |
| Moderate | 160 | 325 | 4–5 |
| Moderately hot | 180 | 350 | 6 |
| Hot | 200 | 400 | 7–8 |
| Very hot | 220 | 425 | 9 |